D0885680

Content Creator

How To Stand Out Amongst The Noise

Myra E. Looring

Table of Contents

Introduction

"We need to stop interrupting what people are interested in and be what people are interested in."

~ Craig Davis

It's 6 AM, and your day has just begun. Like most people these days, one of the first things you'll do is check your phone. You want to know what happened while you were asleep. It feels good starting the day updated on all of the things that interest you. That way, when you walk into the office later today and start working, it won't feel like you live under a rock. Social media is so embedded in our culture that it has become an essential part of our life. Other than massive user numbers, there's one crucial ingredient that powers social media - content!

Our world is evolving, and with that evolution comes the need for adaptation. Even the typical 9 to 5 job has evolved such that there is a large demand for creative people and creative outlets in the workplace. Being creative in today's market means multitasking. Multitasking is the only way you can stand out and become an indispensable asset in our current job market. If you are good at sales, for example, you will also need to become adept at writing. If you are a web designer, you must also enhance your graphic design knowledge.

The two examples above are only a brief glimpse into what the demand for creatives looks like. So, what does this mean for you? For starters, there is so much you can do as a creative. It is fair to say you want to be a successful content creator - everyone does. You have probably watched some videos of top content creators and influencers discussing how much they make in a month. Their salaries are mind-boggling. The beauty of this line of work is that it is passive income. Content creators literally make money while sleeping. If that's not hacking life, then what is?

This book will put you on the right path to mastering content creation mastery. The content market is such a spectacle because there are so many avenues to consider. If you are new to content creation, you may not have heard the phrase "Content is King." By the end of this book, you will understand why this common phrase is actually very true for content creators. In the digital world, content truly is king.

One important guiding principle of content creation is sustainability. While we'll focus on video content creation in this book, sustainability is the common denominator in all of the different content creation niches. It is how your brand becomes a household name. Before you dive into content creation, it is wise to have a solid understanding of your niche beforehand. Use your content as an outlet to showcase the talents you already have.

There's a lot of money in content creation, and you can stake out your corner of the content creation empire. Content creation pays well because it is an art form. Think of yourself as one of the famous painters whose work is displayed in some of the top art galleries in the world. See yourself as Rihanna, performing for millions of fans on SuperBowl Sunday. You have the talent, you have the skills, and you have the platform. Now all you need is the insight to make your bank account reflect your talents.

This is not a sales pitch, nor is it a motivational speech - this is life. As a career marketing consultant, I have helped many individuals and brands come alive through their content. It is so rewarding to help brands refine their content, launch channels, and watch brands grow with their audience. This is where the concept of sustainability comes in.

The modern online audience has a short attention span, and with many brands competing for their attention, the content market can be a savage place. If you are not careful, the content market can crush you and swallow you whole, but of course, we don't want to see this happen to you. Your viewers are your customers. Put yourself in their shoes for a moment. Think of the social media pages you follow religiously. What is it about these pages that keep you coming back? Thinking about this will give you answers that will guide you as you get into content creation.

Other than having engaging, useful content, your audience needs to see you as an authority figure. Authority content is anything that is relatable, insightful, and applicable in people's lives. By providing this type of content, you will manufacture demand for your brand. This is something I have done successfully for more than five years for many different brands. I have nurtured brands from infancy to maturity through content creation, and this work has been one of the most rewarding experiences of my life. From experience, I can tell you that the tips in this book have helped many businesses grow, and I hope to read about your success stories someday, too!

Although it is true that there is already so much content out in the world, this shouldn't unnerve you. People create new content channels every day and still find success. There are many approaches to content creation that you can take, especially when it comes to video content. The influencer market, for example, is incredibly attractive to content creators. Right now, influencer marketing is the "trendy thing" on social media. Top brands are always looking for influencers who can add a new dimension to their marketing strategies. Through video content creation, you can build a name for yourself and position your brand in a way that appeals to clients.

In addition to learning about influencer marketing, this book can also be helpful if you want to diversify your career into the creatives industry. Whether you are starting your brand from scratch or not, you will find useful knowledge in this book to help you position yourself for success. Another way of venturing into the content market is to start your business as a side hustle. You can start by working on a simple project at home in your free time and grow your audience and influence over time.

Many content creators started their brand as a side hustle that eventually turned into a registered business as their brand grew. Others have successfully launched careers in content creation. No matter which of those options appeals to you, sharing your interests, skills, or knowledge with a wider audience has the potential to create great opportunities and open up your world.

Chapter 1:

Want to Be a Content

Creator?

With the rise of the gig economy, many people have ventured into different and innovative fields. One of these fields is content creation, which is a term you probably see frequently on the web. There are many opportunities for content creators. Primarily, a content creator is someone who creates information and shares it with a target audience. Whether the content is educational or entertaining, this information must be captivating and valuable to your audience. When creating content, your emphasis should be on appealing to the audience's interests or helping them overcome challenges. You can create different kinds of content such as eBooks, infographics, photos, blog posts, newsletters, and videos.

Influencers are some of the most popular content creators in the digital sphere. These are people who have gained a huge online following and are considered to be authority figures on their respective topics. Influencers have a tremendous impact on their audiences and this is why they become a household name.

Once you get into content creation, there are endless opportunities for you. Right now, I'm sure that you want to succeed in this sector and become the next big thing. So, what does it take to get there? It will require that you align yourself with the right approach, and you will have to put all your effort into this venture. First, you must decide on the best platform for your content. Will you broadcast on YouTube, post on a blog, or will you use social media platforms like Instagram and Facebook? Eventually, you will also need to think about monetization. Therefore, you should be thinking about a business plan.

A common mistake many content creators make is to rush the process, hoping to strike gold as soon as possible. Your first year in content creation will be about learning the ropes, so it's unlikely that you will make a lot of money in your first year. However, you can still make incredible progress at the beginning of your career. Like all good things, success will not come overnight because it will take time to perfect the art. Here are some useful things you should do that will help you climb the ladder to success faster:

1. Learn more about your audience

The bittersweet truth about content creation is that you are always at the mercy of your audience. This can be a problem, because it means that your audience can dictate your creativity. Unfortunately, you will need your audience to grow and monetize your content. One of your objectives, therefore, should be to study the audience, learn their interests, and in the process, you should find creative opportunities that you can exploit.

Knowing your audience inside-out means understanding their tastes, preferences, problems, and characteristics. Think about factors such as their age group, location, gender, job titles, and any other features that you can use to create definitive clusters.

2. Stay up to date with industry information

Content sustainability is necessary if you want to become a big name in the content market. With sustainability comes the need for relevance. Just like you have to understand your audience, you must also understand the industry. Try and figure out what's currently happening in the industry. By understanding current trends in the industry, you'll be able to put your content into context, which will help you align your content with your objectives.

3. Create a unique vantage point

Lots of content creators will be doing the same kind of thing you do. The worst mistake would be to copy, or make it seem like you are copying, someone's work. Audiences crave authenticity, and if they think that you are inauthentic, your work will be disliked. Presenting original content is one of the challenges that many content creators struggle with.

Remember that you are competing with both big and small content creators, so you must strive to present your work using your personal voice to reach your specific audience. On this note, keep in mind that even though audiences might come to your channel for the content, it will be your personality that keeps them coming back.

4. Grow your network

Successful content creators focus on growth metrics. Your success depends on more than just your passion for your project - you must also network with other content creators. Learn from their mistakes, exchange ideas, and use this knowledge to refine your project.

In terms of growth, you also have to think about your key performance indicators (KPIs). How will you optimize your content and make it easier for your audience to find? KPIs tell you more about your content performance compared to specific expectations that you set. They include organic traffic, traffic from social media, and submissions, which are useful in lead generation.

As you can see, content creation is not a walk in the park. As I mentioned earlier, if you approach this like a business and formulate a business plan, you'll have a much better chance of succeeding. You will learn so much along the way, including social media marketing and how to factor algorithms into your work. All this will go a long way in making your videos and brand visible. Remember that you are not just creating and uploading videos, you are also laying the foundation for what will hopefully become a brand in the foreseeable future.

Demand for Content Creation

The basic business concept of supply and demand applies to content marketing, too. Some people have even labeled video marketing as the future of marketing. If that is true, then the future is now. The dynamics of supply and demand will help you determine if it is prudent for you to invest in video content. Do you have the necessary resources to curate content? Is your target audience large enough to support your future growth? Will all your effort be worth the trouble in the long run?

Content curation is one of the pillars of the digital marketing industry. Whether you want to become an influencer or you want to sell products, you must be an innovative curator. Many businesses today work with content creators to keep their existing customers enticed and to attract new ones to the brand. The idea is to lure in more visitors. Increased traffic to the brand's online outlets means more leads, which could translate to more customers.

More video content is watched online today than ever before. This alone is enough proof that you are investing your time and resources in the right place. From laptops to smartphones, more video content is being consumed in the digital age. This begs the question, what are people watching online?

At a cursory glance, you might assume that the only thing that video audiences want to see is entertainment. This is not true. While it is true that entertainment needs are being met, online video consumption has also increased for other categories. For example, people watch videos to learn more about a brand when they are considering buying a product. With the demand for video content increasing, many influencers have realigned themselves and are now producing quality content to meet that rising demand.

Video is largely in demand because of its unique ability to keep audiences attentive. Think about it, how many times have you fast-forwarded through a podcast or skimmed over an article without actually reading it? Granted, you can also skip through a video recording to find a section that appeals to you, but people will still pay more attention to videos than other forms of media. You can even download the video and watch it later. Therefore, if you want to garner more attention for your brand, video is certainly the way to go.

Let's go a step further and consider social media. Each of the top outlets, Twitter, Facebook, and Instagram, are angling more towards incorporating video content. This is in response to consumer demand. Users engage more with video posts than other types of content. On Twitter, for example, you may come across a fairly unpopular tweet with a video linked to it, yet the video attached to it has received millions of views. This tells you all you need to know about content consumption habits online. Stores on Instagram are currently driving more sales through their video content. Brands have realized that videos are increasingly popular with audiences and that videos have a great influence on consumer decisions.

Taking the aforementioned factors into consideration, you can customize your content curation to get more out of this market. Here are some benefits you might enjoy:

1. Niche mastery

Online audiences have an insatiable hunger for expertise. Each time you produce content, you must market yourself as an expert. This is what people yearn for, and without it, your content will be considered mediocre. Each consumer niche has unique needs that you must meet. This, along with the growing demand for video content, means you must work harder to sell your brand and reap the benefits.

2. Social media growth

Growing your presence on social media is a content creator's dream. As the numbers grow, so does your reputation and the potential for amazing gigs and partnerships. Feeding the consumer demand for videos by creating consistent and intuitive content will provide more opportunities for your brand's growth. What's your endgame? If you are working towards a monetary goal, you must create content that will drive organic traffic. Without organic traffic, you will have to depend on paid advertising, which might not always yield good results.

3. Customer validation

Online customer relationships can be a tricky affair. You want to create long-term relationships. If you create engaging content, you will receive messages from customers talking about something they loved about your videos, or asking questions. This kind of validation makes you a go-to expert on the kind of content you produce.

The ultimate goal when producing video content is to ensure that you become one of the first names that come to mind when something happens in your niche or market. As the digital landscape evolves, you can use videos to capitalize on a variety of market sensors and indicators. Audiences today consume content on the go. Through video content, you can position yourself as an authoritative curator, and align your content in a way that helps you reap the benefits of the increased demand for video content.

Why Video Is Important

Videos offer more value to users, hence their widespread popularity. This especially applies to content that involves lots of processes or movement. You have probably noticed by now that most support, sales, and training teams prefer video content. But, why is video so important?

As previously stated, the popularity of video content is driven by consumer demand. With billions of content watched online every day, YouTube is a great place for content creators. There's a great demand for fresh content in different categories. From entertainment to informational and educational content, there is so much you can work with.

Here are some interesting statistics on online video content consumption (Cooper, 2020):

1. On social media, videos are the most commonly consumed form of media.
2. More than 90% of online users watch videos online at least once per month.
3. In the past month, at least 60% of online users have watched a video on one of the top social media platforms.
4. In terms of popularity, vlogs have now overtaken podcasts.
5. YouTube comes second only to Google as the most popular website in the world, with more than 2 billion monthly visits.
6. More than 1 billion hours of video are watched on YouTube each day.
7. More users are open to learning about a new product or service by watching a video online.

Today, more people would rather watch videos to learn about a product or service than read about that product. As a content creator, your challenge is to create the kind of valuable content that meets the needs of your target audience. So, what sets videos apart from other types of content? The answer lies in the following features that are more accessible in videos than in other forms of content:

1. Emotional appeal

Compared to other forms of content, videos create a stronger emotional appeal to the audience. Through video content, you can communicate different messages and emotions. Videos convey context and have a stronger emotional impact than written words alone. By personalizing the message, you establish an authoritative connection with the audience.

2. Engaging content

We are social beings. For this reason, stories and narratives appeal to our personal values better than any other form of communication. There's no better way to tell a story than through videos. Videos allow the audience to visualize the narrative and even see themselves as part of the story.

3. Empathize with the audience

Audiences seek content that they can relate to. When the viewer can watch someone talk about universal challenges, they will feel comforted and can know that they are not alone. This is the feeling audiences seek when watching videos. Other than showing them how to solve their problems, you will also be showing your viewers that you care. When shooting the videos, authenticity will keep your audience hooked because they will feel that they can trust you.

4. Educational material

The human brain processes visual information faster than text. If you are producing educational content, it makes sense to use videos so that the message is impactful.

From the above statistics, you can begin to understand why more people watch videos today than ever before. Videos are at the forefront of the digital transformation in content consumption. There is so much potential in video marketing, and this is why venturing into this type of content creation will allow you to tap into lots of opportunities.

When producing video content, you should always produce the kind of content that appeals to your audience. Let's have a look at some of the video types you can produce:

1. Vlogs

Your blog might already be amazing, but a video blog will be even better. Vlogs are good landing pages for websites, and they perform well on social media, too. Your vlog is an affordable way to establish your personal image and make your brand's voice appeal to your target audience.

2. Webinars

Virtual seminars have been a hit since the creation of Google+, and in light of the recent pandemic, their popularity has increased. Webinars are a great way of offering practical tips and educating your audience. In modern marketing, this is such a valuable tool to have in your arsenal. You can use webinars to review products, respond to common questions, or even to host a panel discussion of experts in your niche.

3. Presentations

If you want to know how popular video presentations can be, look no further than TED talks. The topics of TED talks are just as intriguing as their speakers are, which makes the global audience eager for the next session. Presentations are exciting and can breathe life into what would have otherwise been just an average webinar.

4. Tutorials

Many YouTube influencers became stars in their niches by making tutorials. You will find a tutorial for virtually anything on YouTube. From gaming to fixing leaking faucets, there's always something you can learn on YouTube. Tutorials are a hit, especially with the millennial generation, because of their practical nature.

5. Interviews

Q&A sessions are a great way of building brand loyalty because, through the interviews, you can align your brand with another brand or person that is held in high regard by your audience. You can use interviews to get the inner scoop on trending topics and you may be able to give your audience exclusive stories.

6. Live streams

People want to consume content as it's being created. The internet population today frowns upon old news. With always news breaking in every part of the world, live streams have become a hit. Whether it's a live stream of a sporting event, breaking news, or a scandalous story, most people want to engage with it as it happens. This desire can also be attributed to FOMO (fear of missing out). Besides, live streams are captivating because the audience doesn't know what will happen next. The fact that they can consume news as it happens, while the story is still in its raw, unedited form, makes live streams kryptonite for online audiences.

There are many other forms of video content that you can push online. Video marketing gives you incredible opportunities to not just engage your audience, but also to build a brand that focuses on your goals and objectives. Ultimately, viewers want compelling content, and if you can provide it, you won't be far from achieving your monetary goals.

Content Creation Benefits

When you think about content creation in terms of all the successful influencers you know, it's easy to assume this is an easy job. Like all other ventures, content creation takes a lot of hard work and dedication. It is not just about uploading your videos. You also must learn your script, edit your video, work with technical crews if you are not producing your own videos, and most importantly, you have to set and meet deadlines. Content creators spend hours on end working on their releases, producing, sharing, and trying to engage audiences. Whether you get into content creation as a full-time or part-time job, you must devote your energy, time, and attention to it.

From the requirements above, it might seem like content creation is just as resource-intensive as any other regular job. So, why should you invest in this? What do you gain from being a content creator? Let's now look at some of the benefits of being a content creator:

1. Great opportunities

Curating content opens your world to incredible opportunities. You have a chance to make a name for yourself online through your content. You can inspire people, teach your audience, express your creativity, and so on. Once your content is uploaded, you have the whole world as your audience, especially if you upload your content on YouTube.

This is not just about creating content, it is also about building a business and making yourself into a brand. The best thing about online content creation is that you have a chance of interacting with the entire world, for free!

2. Earn a steady income

Content creation is one of the top ways that people earn income online today. Whether it be your YouTube channel, blog, or website, content creation offers an opportunity to earn a steady income. You can run ads, earn money through referrals and commission, and so on. There are many young people earning millions of dollars from content creation and influencing online, which should be proof enough that this can be a good opportunity for you. You can create content online as a full-time job or as a side hustle, but as long as you do it right, you are looking at an income-earning opportunity.

You can make money through content creation in many ways. If you have a large following, you can sell merchandise such as mugs, bracelets, and t-shirts. With a huge following, you can also create sellable content like courses, especially if you have an educational channel. Another option for earning money through your channel is through sponsorships and by partnering with leading brands. This way, you can review their products or services and get paid for those reviews.

3. A creative outlet

Content creation offers lots of opportunities for you to bring your creativity to light. Getting in front of the camera allows you to share something unique all the time. You can do so much in content creation; it allows you to express yourself and learn things in the process. The beauty of content creation is that there is so much to learn, and each time you try something new, you'll learn new tricks and tips that make you a better content creator. The longer you keep at it, the more you'll refine your skills and improve.

4. Become a household name

Through your content channels, you can easily become a household name that is synonymous with a specific topic or event. Let's use an example of transfer season in football, for example. While news outlets like Sky Sports will share updates from time to time, football fans will pay attention to transfer updates, negotiations, and proceedings when someone like Fabrizio Romano discusses them. Granted, other personalities in the game produce similar content, but over the years, Fabrizio has set himself above the rest and has become a household name in transfer news. At times, he has even been considered a more reliable source of transfer information than some established media houses.

5. Exit your comfort zone

Nothing pushes you out of your comfort zone in content creation more than video production. Looking at all the content curators in your niche, you know you must go the extra mile to impress audiences. You must keep pushing yourself to do better, and push yourself to become a better content producer. Through video, for example, you try to provide audiences with practical tips on how to solve problems in their lives. This will push you to put yourself in their shoes, understand their challenges, and find solutions that your audience can relate to.

6. Trendy adaptations

Let's face it: videos are the "in-thing" in content creation at the moment. If you are savvy with your social media use, you will realize that most, if not all the top content creators are posting videos from time to time. This is because a video has a powerful ability to engage audiences and keep them hooked.

Content creators who use videos effectively always stand out. From bloggers to established brand outlets, videos will capture the audience's attention better than any other form of content. This explains why social networks like TikTok have grown so rapidly. It is also one of the reasons why there's a new trending challenge on social networks almost every other week.

To sum all these benefits, being a content creator is one of the most powerful skills you can have in the digital marketplace today. Like other powerful positions, you must also exercise responsibility while you have this power. Use your imagination to share ideas, inspire people, champion for change, and share your life and the things you love with the world.

Becoming a Content Creator

It's all fun and games until you realize how huge the task ahead really is. You can take up content creation as a career, but before you do, you must make sure that you know what it entails and prepare yourself for what lies ahead. Maybe you ventured into content creation as a hobby, but over time, you realized that you can take your content creation to the next level. This is where things get challenging because now you must start thinking about formulating a strategy.

There's a big difference between a hobbyist and a professional content creator. While a hobbyist creates content for fun, and usually does so in their spare time, a professional content creator has a plan for everything. You have a plan for audience engagement, your time, resources, and how you will recruit other content creators to work with. Your work is built around goals, targets, and objectives. At this point, you'll start thinking of yourself as a company, a brand whose reputation is on the line.

To get started on the right path, here are some useful tips on how to lay the perfect foundation for success in content creation:

1. Who is your audience?

The first step is to understand your audience. You might get your start as a content creator using sheer luck, but luck is not something you can depend on all the time. Before you shoot a video, think about your audience and what they want. Go over your script as many times as you need to make sure that you are producing something that your audience will consume and enjoy.

Just as there are one-hit wonders in the music industry, the same applies to content creation. You have probably heard of many content creators who produce an amazing video that goes viral, who never make another video afterward. This is because they never planned their brand beyond that viral video.

Before you produce anything, remember that on the other side of the screen is a person who probably knows nothing about you. In this case, the benefit of the doubt will rarely work in your favor. You are competing against top influencers, brand names, and niche content producers. Try to inspire, inform, and impress the audience in your first impression without making your content feel too staged.

2. Work diligently

Content creation is not just about uploading videos, it involves a lot of hard work. This is creative work, and like all forms of art, you must be diligent and smart about it. Writing scripts, recording several takes, discussing your content, and capturing insightful moments on your phone takes a lot of work. At some point, you might even get overwhelmed and need a break. You will also write proposals, and spend long hours brainstorming and refining your story before it is ready to be published.

3. Sharpen your skills

Imagine how much input goes into bringing you some of the top segments on CNN and other channels you follow on TV. Now picture yourself doing all that, with nothing close to the kind of budget that the CNN reporters have. To produce amazing content, you will need to sharpen your journalism, marketing, and writing skills. This is just a start. You must also learn how to speak to and appeal to audiences. This is where your creativity comes in.

There are many content creators out there who have never seen the inside of a university, but still churn great content all the time. How do they do it? Through their storytelling skills. You might be great at writing scripts and may even have a good presence on social media, but that might still not cut it. You must also be comfortable with your soft skills. The secret to your success lies in your ability to communicate and tell your story in a way that moves the audience.

4. Audience engagement metrics

Do not get swayed by the allure of your follower count. This mistake is where many content creators fall short. The most important metric is actually your follower engagement. You can have a huge following online, but only have a handful of them engage with your content. This means that if you are selling something, only a fraction of your audience would be willing to buy that product. In this case, your follower count isn't helping your cause.

To succeed in content creation, you want an audience that interacts not just with your content, but also with you. High engagement means that people respond to your posts, ask questions, and so on. This is why having a huge following might be misleading. Many brands today shy away from creators who have a huge following but have nothing to show for it in terms of engagement. One of the reasons this happens is because some content creators buy their followers. Their follower count, in such a case, will never tell the true story of audience engagement.

Successful content creators know how to pitch their content to audiences, tell a story, and keep them hooked. This is what you are aiming for. Therefore, from the very beginning, focus your effort towards a higher engagement rate instead of a higher follower count. Strive to get your audience commenting and sharing your content because they find value in it.

As you can see, there's a lot of creative energy and hard work that goes into bringing content to life. Aim to create pleasing, engaging, likable content that aligns with your growth strategy that, at the same time, meets the needs of your audience.

Chapter 2:

Before You Start

Content creation is one of the most searched terms on Google today. With different platforms that you can use to upload and share content, there is a huge market for creators. Each content creator hopes to become the next big thing and succeed in the industry. So, with all the competition, how can you ensure that you stand tall in the industry? Let's jump right in with useful tips to help you succeed in your venture:

1. Choosing an appropriate platform

Now that you have brainstormed and have come up with some ideas for your content project, the next step will be to choose where to post your work. There are many platforms where your project can grow. Choosing an appropriate platform means understanding its target audience, and deciding if that platform is suitable for your kind of content.

Take Instagram, for example. Instagram originally marketed itself as a good platform for sharing photos. This set it apart from other social networks. Over time, Instagram has evolved so much that you can now share and promote your videos, too. Since it is a visual-based network, you want to share your content on Instagram, even if you primarily post content on YouTube.

Speaking of YouTube, YouTube should be your go-to platform for video content.

As you are starting your content creation career, make sure that you start on the right foot. Have a solid plan not just for starting your project, but also for how you plan to scale it over time. From the beginning, engage your followers and create a healthy relationship with them. Brands within your niche that seek engagement might recognize your effort and approach you in the future.

2. The audience always comes first

When you start creating content, you must know that it is no longer about you. You have an audience, and everything you do on your platform will always revolve around your audience, their views, and opinions. To keep your audience engaged and excited, you should think about the things that appeal to them. You hope to gain more page views, engagement, growth for your channel, and in the long run, profits from your investment. None of this is possible without your audience.

Ask yourself, what kinds of people would appreciate your content? Once you figure out the demographics, dig deeper, and find out the kind of content that your target audience likes. Think about your competitors in that niche, research, and find out how they present their content. An easy way to learn more about audiences is to read comment sections. You will learn about different opinions, unmet expectations, and suggestions. You can also read the comments on posts shared by your competitors.

Listening to your audience and addressing their needs will create the kind of rapport that will help you grow a huge following. This, in the long run, increases your chances of getting more revenue from the channel through ads and sponsorships.

3. Content relevance

Everywhere you go today, you'll find someone with a blog, website, or YouTube channel with content similar to what you are offering. This creates a big challenge - how to become and stay relevant in the industry. You can go about this in several ways. Ultimately, your audience needs relevant content, and they need it at the right time. To stay ahead of the pack, make a habit of uploading fresh, current content.

The digital world moves at such a fast pace that you cannot afford to upload stale news. People will always search for the latest news, and each time your channel offers what they are looking for, your authority status rises in the minds of your audiences. If, for example, you have a food channel, try to review new restaurants before anyone else. Sample new menus and talk about them on your channel. Adventurous eaters and revelers will soon flock to your channel for recommendations.

4. Release fresh content regularly

At this point, you should be thinking about yourself not just as an individual, but as a brand or a business entity. To see growth, you must upload content regularly. People need to see some consistency in your work, or they will move on to the next best thing.

Since you might not be able to physically post all the time at the same time, you can think of a content schedule. With a good plan, you can schedule posts in advance, so that your audience will never miss your posts, especially for those who look forward to new content.

Your content and skills notwithstanding, due diligence is necessary if you are to succeed in content creation. Note that content creation is not one of the get rich quick or overnight schemes you read about all the time. This is a serious venture that requires your hard work, dedication, and persistence.

Basic Content Creation Skills

Everyone talks about starting a YouTube channel all the time, but very few make it. With more content creators flocking YouTube and other video sharing platforms, you must go beyond the tips discussed above to succeed. You might not even know the identities of most of your competitors, yet you all fight for the audience's attention. Below, we will look at the basic skills necessary for content creation, especially on YouTube.

1. Operating recording devices

Every newbie on the internet records something on their smartphone, uploads it and it goes viral. This works, but only for a while. You cannot rely on your phone all the time, and since you are going into this as a professional content creator, you need to think big.

From the very beginning, you must get the video resolution right. Everyone appreciates high-quality video, so you should be thinking in terms of HD resolution and at least 1080p. At this resolution, you get fascinating colors. By the time of this publication, more devices support 4K so you should also think along that line, especially if you want your content to have a longer shelf life. However, note that at 4K, the sizes are larger and will take longer to upload. On the same note, you need a good quality laptop or computer to edit 4K videos comfortably.

You must also get the color profile right when recording. Whether you are using a mirrorless or DSLR camera, the right color profile can help you enhance the output. You can also record some scenes in black and white. This comes in handy when you want to express a unique vibe or mood. It might take a bit of experimenting to find the right mood for your story, so take your time with it.

Another feature you should look into when producing content especially for YouTube audiences is the frame rates, measured in frames per second (fps). While the average video records at 30fps, most people use 24fps to deliver that cinematic experience. As technology advances and consumers access better quality devices and internet speeds, some content creators go a notch higher with 60fps. While this is great for those who have high-tech devices, it might be a challenge for those who use average devices. However, there is one benefit of recording at 60fps that you might enjoy - you can slow down the recording and get that cinematic experience too. Besides, depending on your budget, you can get cameras that can shoot at 120fps. If one of your scenes is better shot in slow motion, 120 fps would be ideal.

2. Video editing skills

Unless you plan to upload the raw video as recorded on your phone or camera, you need to learn some video editing skills. Luckily today there are lots of programs and applications that can help with this. Of course, you want to edit out the intruders, photobombers, and those parts of the recording where you ran out of content and filled in with *"um"*'s. While editing the recording, you can also adjust the frame rate, add, edit, or remove some content to ensure your video delivers the right message and in the desired mood.

If you are just starting out and without a sizable budget you can edit videos on your phone. There are many apps for this, with iMovie being one of the top picks especially for iPhone users. For Android users, there are lots of options available in the app store such as Filmorago, Luma Fusion, and Power Director.

Editing on your phone is easy, but might not be appropriate for some projects. For bigger projects, a laptop or your computer will be much better. For this too, there are lots of editing programs you can use, including Adobe Premiere Pro, Vegas Movie Studio, and Filmora. You are, however, not limited to these programs. There are lots more that are suitable for different skill levels, from beginner to professional.

If you find it difficult to use any of the programs, you can find tutorials on how to use them on YouTube. Other than that, you can also find expert tutorials on learning sites like Udemy. The few hours you spend learning will pay off in the future, so give it a try!

3. Light and background settings

How many times have you watched an interesting video but somewhere in the middle, you got distracted by a sudden drop in quality, or you felt the uploader could have done better? A common reason for this is because many uploaders either don't know how to set the appropriate light setting for their videos, or they get overzealous and push their limits. Poor lighting will always affect the recording quality, regardless of your editing skills. If you shoot a video under terrible lighting, there's very little you can do to improve it since the original content is poor.

Natural light is always a sure bet when shooting videos. However, this might also mean you are restricted to filming during the day and hope the sun shows up for your gig. Since you won't always enjoy the luxury of natural lighting, you must improvise where applicable. So, how do you go about this?

Invest in studio lighting. The options here are endless and available for any budget. Most content creators use the ring light when starting out. It is affordable, portable and you can even attach it to your phone. You can also get a large ring light that you attach on a tripod. Other than the ring light, LED panel lights and softboxes are also popular. As you delve deeper into content production, you might advance into RGB LED lights that cast a variety of colors in the background.

4. Recording audio

Your videos might be amazing, but if you cannot get the audio in sync, all your effort will be futile. People are often captivated by the visual antics that they forget about the audio. For storytelling purposes, you must give audio the attention it deserves. There is so much that goes into audio recordings, so let's look at them briefly.

First, unless you have express approval from the owner, do not use copyrighted audio in your recording. This is the easiest way to get your videos taken down on YouTube. There are lots of copyright-free music you can use as background tunes. Choose tunes that are appropriate with your video, that will not distract the audience. Try out different tunes until you find the perfect fit. Brainstorming will come in handy here.

Are the voices audible? Is the music too loud it drowns the conversation? These are some of the important things most beginner content creators overlook. For a start, the average audio recording on your smartphone might work well. However, investing in a micro microphone you can attach to your device will deliver better quality.

If you are recording with a mirrorless camera or DSLR, note that most of these don't have the best audio features, so you must invest in an external microphone. A lapel microphone (lavalier) or shotgun microphone works perfectly if you are using any of these cameras. If your budget allows, there are lots of audio recording equipment you can use.

5. Creating effective thumbnails

Thumbnails are often overlooked by many beginner content creators, whose emphasis is often limited to the video recording. Most platforms like YouTube will assign a thumbnail frame by default if you don't create one. This is a gamble you should never take because the default thumbnail frame might not reflect the video quality you want.

Thumbnails give the audience a quick preview of the video. Think of thumbnails as putting your ad on a billboard. You want the viewers to be wowed instantly. For this reason, use vibrant colors, and ensure you choose an appropriate theme that can sell your video. There are many free or affordable apps you can use to create effective thumbnails.

The skills above are essential for creating amazing video content. However, note that they can only help you make a good script better. These are technical aspects of video production that you must take into consideration. That aside, you must ensure you have quality content before you even think of the production essentials.

Video Recording Equipment

Video creation is not as easy as the outcome makes it seem. You have the content, personality, and everything else going for you. The next step is having the right equipment for the job. Gone are the days when all you had to do was record something simple with your smartphone. The content space gets more competitive by the day, so you cannot afford to start on the wrong footing. Indeed, there's a steep learning curve, but you don't have to go through it. You want to give your audience the best viewing experience from the beginning. For starters, you don't have to hire an expert team or purchase professional recording equipment. Below is the basic equipment you need for video production:

1. Camera

A good camera is one of the first things you want to get your hands on. There are many brands out there, so you need to know what you are looking for. Because you are just starting out, you don't have to go for the most expensive camera in the stores either. You can find amazing quality cameras for the right price when you are just beginning your career. Most content creators start with their smartphones and upgrade to quality cameras as they work their way in the industry.

With many factors to consider in terms of camera selection, always consider the kind of content you are creating when choosing cameras. Bearing this in mind, you can choose from any of the following:

- **Webcams**

Webcams are a hit with many beginner content creators because they are affordable. They are easy to use since most of them are plug and play, making them an ideal option in case you are recording in front of your computer. Webcams are, therefore, a good option if you record and upload gaming videos. If you run a live streaming channel, webcams will come in handy.

There are many variants in the market, so you have several features to consider. A good webcam should feature support for full HD in 1080p, have an independent processor through which it can process content instead of burdening your computer processor, which will slow you down.

- **Camcorders**

Camcorders are specifically built to record videos, making them an ideal option for YouTube content creation. Modern models are affordable, portable, compact, and sturdy enough to shoot in any location.

When looking for a reliable camcorder, check to ensure it has an image stabilization feature. This is important because it will reduce blurring and shaking if you are shooting in handheld settings. You should also look for a camcorder that can shoot in 1080p and up to around 60fps. Most models today are built to sync to the cloud, so you can upload content to the internet instantly.

- **Mirrorless camera**

Content creators fell in love with the mirrorless camera because it gives them the same performance you can get from a DSLR, without the bulkiness. Because of their small and light form factor, these cameras are a hit in the industry as they are portable, making them ideal for recording content at home, or on the go.

- **Action camera**

Action cameras are versatile, hence among some of the most reliable cameras in the game. You can use them to capture different types of shots and are a good fit for sporting shots and first-person point of view shots. They are practical devices, and their small size notwithstanding, you can produce some amazing content with them. Because they are durable and also for the content quality, many content creators on YouTube use action cameras.

- **DSLR**

Content creators on YouTube love these cameras because they deliver the best quality. The fact that you can use them in low light conditions makes them a plus in case you are shooting in a location that doesn't give you the luxury of proper lighting. The video recording quality is incredible, and from the clarity, you can see why many content creators love it on YouTube. If you are serious about your YouTube career and want to take it to the next level, owning a DSLR will be one of the best investments ever.

2. Microphone

You have the camera in check, so the next step is to find the right microphone. Many people lose engagements on YouTube because their audio and video are not in sync. You might have the best video production, but as long as your audio does not match its quality, your work will never impress audiences. Terrible audio is a common reason why people give horrible reviews on videos online.

Your camera or your laptop might have built-in microphones, but they do not deliver the kind of quality you would want to share with your audience. They cannot clear ambient sounds from the background, neither can they deliver proper recording features. For this reason, invest in a good quality microphone for your work. Let's have a look at some of the top options you have in the market right now:

- **USB Microphone**

USB microphones are the height of simplicity. Not so long ago, these microphones were largely unheard of. However, today you will find many YouTube content creators with them. One of the reasons why they are popular is because they are affordable. They are easy to use, versatile, and deliver good quality sound.

- **Shotgun microphone**

These come highly recommended if you are recording with small professional cameras. They are popular because they deliver high-quality recordings. To reduce ambient noise, they come with shock mounts, so the mechanical vibrations that come from the microphone do not interfere with the production.

Another reason why they are highly regarded is that you can focus them to capture clear vocals and sounds directly in front of the microphone. This makes them a perfect tool for outdoor recording because they can minimize natural outdoor noise.

- **Condenser microphone**

The condenser microphone comes with volume control and an in-built headphone that allows for self-monitoring so you don't need a pre-amp. Most of these microphones come with mix control built-in, allowing you to blend pre-recorded audio with microphone audio. They are perfect for podcasts and home recordings because of their extended frequency response.

- **Lapel microphone**

This is a wireless model that you can use discreetly, attached to your belt or clothes. You have seen them in TV interviews and reality TV shows. They also come with a transmitter and receiver which help in relaying the signal especially when you are communicating over distances. If you produce content outdoors, you must consider the signal length, and choose a lapel microphone that is reliable over a hundred meters.

3. Gimbal stabilizer or Tripod

When you venture into video production, the last thing you should put your audience through is unsteady footage. It is an avoidable distraction that you can manage using gimbal stabilizers and tripods. At the top of your list, these will improve your video production abilities.

Of the two items, the tripod is the most affordable, with quite a variety available below $100 but offers the best performance. You should, however, choose a tripod based on the overall weight of your camera setup. If resources are not an issue, you can go big on tripods and buy something that will serve you longer and safely support your equipment.

Considering the average YouTuber's needs, look for a tripod that can rise to at least five feet and hold at least ten pounds in terms of camcorder or DSLR weight. The height consideration is important because it allows you flexibility in shooting angles.

However much you try to hold the camera steady, you will still end up with jarring or shaky videos especially if you are shooting from a handheld device. This is where gimbals come in. They have unique stabilizers fitted with weights or motors, which help you get a smooth recording or give a better balance to your camera while in use. Gimbals are ideal for content creators who use lightweight cameras or those who record lots of motion content.

4. Perfect light setting

You have to get the perfect light setting to deliver quality content. If you will be recording content in a poorly lit environment, you must invest in proper lighting equipment. Even in cases where you shoot in areas with proper ambient light, you can still use the lighting equipment available to alter the mood and cast even brightness onto the setup. The following are some types of lighting equipment you can use for content production:

- **Softbox**

Content creators prefer softboxes because they give the closest emulation of natural light, especially from a window. The white diffusion panel built into the softbox helps to manage the intensity of harsh, direct light. A softbox is generally a good option if you want more light in production without worrying about shadowy scenes all over the place.

- **Ring light**

Ring lights are common in the vlogging space. Because of the ring shape, it emits light all around the main subject. Ring lights are efficient in eliminating shadows from all directions. By eliminating shadows, they help to enhance the subject in front of the camera. This explains why this type of camera is so common with fashion, makeup, and beauty vloggers. Ring lights illuminate the face, getting rid of shadows that might highlight the subject's flaws.

- **Umbrella light**

Umbrella lights are common with many content creators because they are affordable. Their portable nature makes them a bold option for many producers, especially when they need soft lighting on set. Umbrella lights are often preferred over softboxes because you get more control over the reflected lights. The lights are controlled from the inner layer of the umbrella. They might not have the diffusion sheet like the softboxes, but they cast light over a large area, making them perfect for shooting on location or creating the perfect backdrop.

- **On-camera lights**

This is a set of continuous lighting that you can mount on cameras. They are perfect for content that requires a lot of exposure, like a birthday, wedding, or documentary videos. They also come in handy when shooting videos in poorly lit settings.

5. Editing programs

We have covered the technical aspects of content production. Up to this point, you have shot and saved some quality content. However, you cannot upload videos in the raw format. You need reliable editing software to deliver the best outcome. YouTube has an in-built video editor, but it has limitations that hinder your creativity. You should be able to edit your videos whichever way you want them, and that is where video editors come in handy. There are several editing programs available in the market, so we will only select a few that come highly recommended, and discuss them in the next section.

Video Editing Programs

As technology advances to match internet speed and audience interest, video marketing keeps growing to match this demand. If you plan to make videos and share with a wide audience, you must also get your hands on the best video editing programs in the market. You don't necessarily need to buy high-end programs, given that you are probably just starting out. We will look at some of the best video editing programs you can use, and why you should pick one over the others.

The best thing about video editing software is that the market is flooded with so many that you don't need to enroll in an expensive course to master them either. Once you start using these programs, you will realize that video editing is not as difficult as most people make it out to be. Here are some programs you can look into:

1. Shotcut

Shotcut comes highly recommended because it is a cross-platform suite. You can install and use it on Linux, Mac OS, and Windows. This kind of flexibility sets it in the right spot for many content creators because they are not limited to a given ecosystem. You can produce content in one machine and continue editing in another, the underlying operating system notwithstanding.

It offers the kind of services you would expect from high-end editing software. You can edit video and audio together on the same timeline, applying captions and effects where applicable. Once you are through, the conversion process to the final video file is seamless. One of the intuitive features built into this program is the drag and drop functionality that makes your work easier especially when dealing with several files.

Shortcut stands out because of its innovative, customizable menu. You also get lots of filters you can use to modify settings and options to enhance your outcome. Task mobility is another feature that allows you to revert to any stage of the editing process. This way, you don't have to undo all your saved work to get back to a distinct point. For easy work, you can share the program on different monitors, allowing you to overcome the challenge of working on different tabs on one computer, which eventually slows down your system. For all the benefits, Shotcut falls short because you cannot preview filters on the platform.

2. Filmora 9

If you have used Windows Movie Maker before, Filmora steps in as a better alternative. This suite comes with everything you need to produce the best content. Filmora allows you flexibility in creating any kind of movie or video. It is packaged with lots of filters, overlays, transitions, elements, custom captions, audio and visual effects that you can use to enhance your content.

As more people get into content creation, the need for mobile video editing programs arose and Filmora has not disappointed them. The mobile platform, Filmora

Go works well in case you need to edit clips on your phone and upload it to YouTube. This makes work easier for you because you can easily create content, edit and upload on the go. The program supports 4K video resolution, and multiple video formats, which makes it easier for you to share content to different platforms. It also comes with a sound music library from which you can get awesome background music for your content. The only caveat when using Filmora is that the free version comes with a branded watermark.

3. Lightworks

Unlike most programs on this list, Lightworks is a free program that works across Mac OS, Linux, and Windows. It is an ideal platform for content creators, sound engineers, camera operators, bloggers, and vloggers. It is such a convenient program, you can use it for home videos, producing content for social networks, or for advertising material.

If your content project is small or you have a low budget, Lightworks would be a great option. It is so easy to work with, allowing you to import and render content in the background, move editing videos, and even create custom keyboard shortcuts to ease the editing process.

This cross-platform program supports multiple features, 3D processing, multichannel support, and more importantly, you can edit and crop videos directly from the timeline. While this is an easily accessible program, the editor management system has often proven difficult for most beginner content creators to use.

4. Adobe Premiere Pro

The Adobe suite has always been the go-to editing suite, not just for content creators, but for many other creatives, especially in graphic design. You can do so much with Adobe Premiere, including modifying colors, adjusting the video, and processing audio content. Adobe Premiere comes with a host of video editing features that you can use to process and modify whichever type of multimedia content you record. The best thing is that you can use the suite on both mobile devices and PCs. You can also run it on Windows, Mac OS, and iOS. This versatility is one of the reasons why many content creators find it reasonably reliable.

For more features, you can always subscribe to the Pro version which includes support for 4K video resolution and 360 VR. With these features, you can use Adobe Premiere for professional video editing services. Considering the features bundled into it, Adobe Premiere is a great tool for beginners and experts alike.

Another reason why it ranks high among the best video editing programs is that the user interface is easy to work with. From here, you can easily export finished projects to a different device in any of the formats acceptable. If you use the complete Adobe suite, you can also upload and integrate content with any other Adobe products.

The performance and ease of use notwithstanding, Adobe Premiere is still one of the most expensive products in the market if you have to pay for the official license.

5. Apple iMovie

Apple products have a reputation for offering simplicity and elegance. For video editing, iMovie offers quality services acceptable to beginners and experts alike. iMovie is so popular it is the go-to video editor for iPad, iPhone, and Mac OS users. Apart from the video editing particulars, iMovie also comes with different music themes, complete with video filters, tiles, and transmissions. You also have access to some amazing effects you can use to enhance your production.

Using iMovie, you can use other features like fast forward, split-screen, slow motion, and image-in-image display. To help you get more flexibility in production, you can use the soundtrack tools available with iMovie. The *Green Screen* in iMovie is similar to the green screen used in professional production houses. Using this screen, you create whichever background you want for your subject, and even switch up locations as you see fit.

iMovie supports 4K resolution, theater mode for video sharing across any devices you connect to your Apple account. More importantly, it has an amazing user interface that makes work easier for content creators. One challenge with iMovie, however, is that it lacks sufficient features to support 360-degree videos and motion tracking.

6. Final Cut Pro X

This is a unique video editor designed by Apple for the Mac OS. Since it's an Apple product, you will notice interface similarities to iMovie. Using this program, you can create amazing video, audio, title, and transition effects. Apart from these basic effects, you can also play around with some of the extra effects to give your videos that pop that gets viewers excited each time you upload a new video.

One of the perks of using Final Cut is that you can integrate video uploads to Vimeo Facebook, and YouTube. It also supports multiple output formats for video content. Final Cut does not come cheap, but considering all the features, it is worth every penny. All the projects are produced in high resolution, which is ideal when uploading videos to YouTube.

Unlike other video editing programs, Final Cut comes with a library from where you can access your current and recent works. From the library, you can also preview effects without appending them to files. This feature will save you a lot of time that would have otherwise been wasted in editing and undoing features. You can also edit videos without losing the image quality in the process.

7. HitFilm Express

This is a free program, so you can give it a shot when you are just starting. If you love the services, you can upgrade to a paid version with extra services. The video processing tools packed into HitFilm alongside the in-built templates give you the easiest no-effort editing experience. HitFilm Express is a hit with many beginners not just because it is free, but also because you can export content in high quality.

Other than clip trimming, you will also enjoy using the color adjustment feature, and export content to different sites in whichever video format you love. The free version also allows you to use green screen keys, create video masks, and use the 3D features to create the most powerful video footage ever.

Using HitFilm Express, you can upload and produce content in 4K and it also supports 360-degree content. In terms of flexibility, you are so far limited to using the program only on Windows and Mac. That notwithstanding, you will enjoy an amazing timeline editor and innovatively flexible video export functions.

8. Adobe Premiere Rush

Initially released for the iOS, Adobe Premiere Rush is an ideal video editing program for tablets and mobile phones. For this purpose, it is a watered-down version of Adobe Premiere Pro. The target market for this program is vloggers and YouTube content creators. The fact that you can record, edit, and upload videos from your mobile or tablet device is great for many content creators. With this, you don't have to invest in an expensive equipment setup.

Some of the features you will enjoy using this app include resizing videos, color correction, editing audio, and lots of other amazing features. With professional templates, you can create quality effects on video titles and share them on social media.

Apart from the easy and fast editing support, this program is fully optimized for social networks, such that you can instantly share your finished works with your fans. The interface is easy to use, and using the sound editing features, you can look forward to releasing amazing content. The only downside of using this app is that it lacks most professional video processing features you'd find in other apps.

9. Blender

Blender is a great editor for content creators producing 3D graphics. It is a popular program with many content creators because of cross-platform compatibility. Other than that, its source code is open source, meaning that you can tweak the program to suit your needs. The functionality and availability make it a great program for content creators and 3D modeling experts.

An interesting fact about Blender is that it is inherently not a video editing app. However, it is still a powerful tool you can use for all your video processing needs. You might, however, run into problems using it because it supports a limited number of file types, so you might also have a difficult time exporting some videos.

It features an intuitive and detailed timeline, and with the audio mixing support, you can create some amazing audio mixes using Blender. You can also enjoy the live preview, filters, and lots of great transitions that can add some personality to your content.

10. Corel VideoStudio

The simplicity in Corel VideoStudio is one of the reasons for its popularity. You have access to so many video editing tools, so simple that beginner content creators can also have a field time with them. It comes with amazing video collage templates, through which you can merge different videos in one format. This is a good feature especially for action camera videos because you can do away with the distortion that is common when editing such videos.

A useful feature in this app is that you can edit and instantly upload content to YouTube. Other than that, you will also enjoy the VR support, 4K resolution, and motion tracking. For rendering purposes, Corel VideoStudio is one of the fastest editing programs you will find in the market.

You have a music library from where you can select copyright-free music for video production. Multicam editing is another feature that makes it stand out from other products. Corel VideoStudio is a great tool for beginner content creators. However, it is lacking in many professional features you would need as you advance your content creation career.

You can use any of the programs above to create some amazing content on YouTube. Like many life skills, you need lots of practice in video editing to go from beginner to expert content production. You can start with some simple videos saved on your smartphone to get a feel of what it takes to use any of these programs.

At the end of the day, do not forget that you are creating a brand. Your audience will benefit from beautiful, smooth, and professional video production. With all the tools available at your disposal, you can rest assured other content creators are pushing their limits.

As you compete for the same audience, make sure you give them your best effort. Quality work is amazing and leaves a lasting impression on your audience. You need good reviews, ratings, and engagement. You can only achieve this when you have great content for the audience.

Chapter 3:

Choosing a Niche

You have come across the words niche marketing more times than you can remember. Carving out a niche from the wider market is not an easy feat. However, for all your effort, the benefit of finding your niche is that you limit your scope to a specific demographic, or address a particular need. Each business has a target audience, within which there exists niches - even smaller groups with unique preferences, needs, and wants. Such groups are often a good source of opportunities. Niche marketing is a marketing approach that focuses on these specific groups.

In content creation, choosing your niche well helps you establish the right direction and focus. There is so much to consider when selecting the right niche. The idea here is to ensure that all your video campaigns are efficient, which will return a higher engagement rating. To get you started, the outlet where your videos will be posted will also determine how well the audience interacts with your content.

Niches are driven by competition. Depending on the industry, you will always find hundreds if not thousands of content creators competing for the same space with you. By targeting a narrower niche, you effectively set yourself away from some of that competition. This also allows you enough room to explore different ideas and challenge the niche market with your content to test their responsiveness.

Niche targeting is a specific objective that allows for flexibility in meeting your goals. Once you figure out the dynamics of your niche, you can easily expand your target outwards from the niche to the general market audience.

How to Choose a Hosting Platform

To succeed in content creation, you must understand why it makes sense uploading content to one platform and not the others. This is important because the chosen hosting platform in a way determines how well your videos will perform. Let's look at some of the key factors you should consider:

1. Streaming Quality

Videos do better with amazing streaming quality. Granted, the audience might have slow internet, making it sensible to access your videos in 480p. However, 1080p should be the minimum for any content platform worth your time. Even if you are working with a limited budget, you should be able to upload videos in 1080p.

Before you upload content to any platform, ensure they support Ultra HD and above. This allows your audience flexibility in their viewing options. Such functionality comes down to the kind of servers that the hosting platform uses.

2. Content Management

The platform you choose should allow you full control over your videos once you upload them. You don't have to worry about third-party control over your content, imposing waiting times, or having to seek approval to upload or edit your work. How much access or privileges do you enjoy as an amateur or professional content uploader?

3. Video Analytics

Your content is uploaded with the audience in mind, so it makes sense that you must find a way to measure audience engagement. For this reason, ensure the platform you choose offers several analytics options. In terms of analytics, you are not just looking at the basics like the number of comments or views on the video, but go deeper into features like the average time people spend watching your video.

With in-depth analytics, you can learn more about audience engagement, like how viewers arrive at your video, the search terms they use, and the point at which they stop watching the video. This is useful information that can help you refine your content for better engagement in the future. As long as your content is live, you should know the reasons why it is a success or why it is not doing well.

4. Advertising

For most content creators, the design of the hosting platform and the ease of customization are some of the important things they look at. However, if you wish to monetize your content, you have to consider the advertising features too. You want to ensure you upload content to a platform that allows you to place ads. Do they allow banner ads or video ads? Where are the ads placed?

Why are such matters important in your decision making? Take YouTube, for example. If you are uploading short videos, YouTube is not the best place for you. Say your content is a 30-second clip, it would not make sense for anyone to watch it, and at the same time, watch a 30-second ad attached to it. For slightly longer videos, however, YouTube would suffice.

5. Security features

Account security seems like something so obvious yet many content creators take it for granted. In this case, let's move away from the basics, of securing your account details and focus on your videos. How secure is your content on that website? You want to upload content on a site where people cannot easily download the videos. The emphasis here is to note the difference between usage and exposure. Ideally, you don't want people to download your videos. That way, they can use it as they please. Instead, you want your audience exposed to the videos. Let them watch your content and keep coming back to watch it whenever they need it.

With all the different workarounds for downloading content, you need a platform that has strict download rules. However, you cannot control what people do on their computers, so there's a good chance your work will still be downloaded regardless of the platform. What next? Think of copyright regulations. Find a platform where you can easily report copyright violations in case someone downloads and uses your content without your permission.

When you are looking for a video hosting platform, there are many factors you should consider. The factors discussed above are, however, the most basic that will not just inform your decision but will also ensure your audience gets a good viewing experience.

Video Hosting Platforms

The right video sharing platform should be a suitable match for yours and your audience's needs. There are many platforms to choose from, and for the same reason, several factors to consider. Some factors you should look at include how often you upload content, your budget, the desired viewing experience for your audience, and how you intend to use the video once you upload it. Let's jump right in and discuss the top hosting platforms:

1. YouTube

YouTube is the grandfather of video hosting. You don't need a license to create a library from videos available to the public, nor do you need to pay for hosting. All you need is a Google account, create your channel, and start uploading videos.

YouTube is a leader in this sector because it doubles up as a video hosting platform and a search engine. In fact, it only ranks second to Google in search engines, reaching more 18-49-year-olds than any cable TV network or broadcast network in the world. With more young people working towards becoming YouTubers in the future, you should position your content to take advantage of this privilege.

Besides, the fact that YouTube is a Google company means that your videos will rank even higher on Google and benefit from the search algorithms. You can also use the same SEO tactics to rank your content higher on YouTube and Google.

For all its greatness, YouTube does have a few drawbacks too. For instance, YouTube is specifically built to keep audiences on it much longer. The average person spends at least 40 minutes watching videos on the platform in a session. The algorithms suggest videos to audiences to keep them hooked, not just on your channel, but on YouTube in general. This means that while someone might come to your channel to watch your video, they might not stay there long enough. This makes it difficult to get and maintain people's attention. Therefore, YouTube might not be a reliable option for converting or engaging users.

Another YouTube challenge is that the recommendation algorithms could easily suggest competitor products or services.

2. DailyMotion

At a cursory glance, you can be swayed by the fact that DailyMotion receives more than 300 million active users each month. Because of such figures, the platform is great for ads. However, as much as you can monetize content on DailyMotion, users have in the past complained about the ad overload. The audience is smaller compared to YouTube, and with their ads being more intrusive, the user experience leaves a lot to be desired. Therefore, in terms of engagement and profitability, you should not expect YouTube-level returns.

Unfortunately, DailyMotion restricts uploads to 60 minutes, so if your content is longer, this would not work for you. Given how intrusive their ads are, they also have upload limitations to counter spam uploaders.

3. JW Player

JW Player has often been considered a YouTube alternative, especially since the earliest YouTube version was hosted on their technology. This is one of the reasons why it has maintained its position as one of the go-to video hosting platforms.

One of the benefits of using JW Player is that you can host videos on the site but cast it elsewhere, like on Facebook. Facebook generally limits you by locking hosted content to its platform. You can bypass this with JW Player. You also get the benefit of real-time analytics on user engagement in terms of their location, devices used, and domains. JW Player is not free. Access starts at $12 a month and rises to $50 a month when you exceed 50,000 plays.

4. Vimeo

Vimeo allows embedded website videos, making it ideal for content creators who wish to send content to specific audiences, for example, those who pay for access. By allowing you to embed videos, you can encourage viewers to fill a form, allowing access to viewers who have paid access and hiding content from those who have not paid.

By design Vimeo was built to support the technical elements of video hosting, making it ideal for content creators who upload paid courses. You can use the free Vimeo service, limiting you to uploading up to 10 videos daily, with the size capped at 500MB a week. The hosting plans are charged monthly. However, note that if you upgrade to a paid account and revert to a free account, you might lose all videos previously uploaded.

5. Loom

Loom is primarily a platform for sharing your screen and not a video sharing platform by design. For this reason, the only videos you can upload to their server must be recorded through Loom. Given its design Loom is perfect for product demonstrations and internal training purposes.

Screen recordings are automatically uploaded onto the platform, with a link you can share with your audiences. Loom is so easy to use, you don't even need a browser for access if you have the desktop app installed. While you can record and host up to 100 videos for free, this is only in standard video quality. You can, however, access the editing suite and upgrade to HD quality uploads for $10 a month.

6. TikTok

This is a video sharing platform where users can share 15-second videos on anything. It started as Musical.ly before it was sold to ByteDance in 2018. TikTok is popular with content creators because it supports localized content even though it is a global platform. Using local hashtags, content creators can jump onto local trends, contests, and challenges to promote their work.

7. OnlyFans

OnlyFans is one of the most popular subscription-based video sharing platforms, probably notorious because of, and popularized by the adult content hosted on it. OnlyFans helps creators monetize content and influence. With more than 30 million users and more than half a million content creators, it is an ideal platform that brings you closer to your audience.

The beauty of OnlyFans is that you can upload anything that wouldn't normally be allowed on other content sharing or hosting platforms. While the adult content is huge on this platform due to its lack of restrictions, many other professionals monetize their content here, including fitness instructors, chefs, and artists.

8. Hosting on your website

Having looked at some of the top hosting platforms, you are probably thinking, *why not just host my videos on my site?* Thanks to HTML5 you can easily host content on your website without using Flash plugins. The latest versions of the modern web browsers like Chrome, Firefox, and Safari support HTML5 video code.

Given this possibility, why does it still make sense to use third-party hosting? Internal hosting will slow down your website speed. The last thing your audiences want is a slow website. This might see you lose engagements over time. Besides, as appealing as self-hosting sounds, you need an elaborate analytics set-up to make it work seamlessly. There is also the fact that people don't always update their websites all the time. Therefore, anyone using older browser versions might be locked out of enjoying your content. Hosting platforms like YouTube have an elaborate distribution network that you cannot enjoy through self-hosting.

In terms of video hosting, you should not limit yourself to one platform. You can consider the logistics involved and optimize your content for different sharing platforms. The idea of a "best hosting platform" is, therefore, subjective depending on your content needs.

Importance of Niche Marketing

Niches are the backbone of the content creation industry. When you figure out your niche, you can use your expertise in the field to help you stand out from the competition. You might have lots of other products and services, but your niche is where you specialize, setting yourself apart from everyone else.

The dynamics of understanding your niche can help you grow your business in three ways. First, you can market content only to your niche. This is a limited view, but is worthwhile if your content, products, or services are a specialty that is only appreciated by a select community. Another option is to market both to the niche and the larger audience. In this case, you must ensure the niche offering is slightly different from the market offering. Finally, you can market to the target audience, but with a niche approach.

While niche marketing might not always work in all business ventures, figuring out your niche dynamics in the content industry is a priceless gem. Below are some reasons why niche content is important for your brand:

1. Better customer relationships

One of the perks of niche content is that you target a specific set of clientele. Depending on your services or products, you might be serving a small market. A small market means that you generally interact with few people. You have a better chance of understanding them better, engaging them deeper and this leads to quality relationships.

There is nothing better for your business than knowing your customers in-depth. By nurturing such relationships, you can personalize communication, make diligent follow-ups, and send personalized appreciation notes to your customers. On the business end, you can also receive special requests from your customers and address them at premium rates.

The practices above can help you create amazing relationships with your customers. You serve them better and enrich your relationships. On the other hand, customers will be loyal to your brand.

2. Stand out from the competition

Products or services that are highly specific generally have fewer companies trying to compete for the same market. The more specific your offering is, the fewer brands compete for customer attention and even fewer brands that might duplicate your content strategy.

While fewer competitors might be good for you, it is not always a good thing in the long run. Lack of competition means that you will spend less time worrying about what other brands are doing, and you might get to a point where you feel so invincible, you stop offering quality services to your audience. This is the point where another brand taps into your market and runs you out of the game. Reduced competition is great, but only if the market is adequate.

3. Brand visibility

Niches are great for visibility. You do not just enjoy easy access to customers, but you also have the benefit of improving your presence online. Niche-serving brands are generally unique. For example gluten-free bakeries or carpet cleaners who only use natural cleaning products. As long as you have a unique selling point, your content will always stand out.

The idea behind niches and visibility is that you should strive to get in front of the right audience all the time. Making your content available to the right audience means they will find and appreciate its value. They will also share your content widely, which works well for your overall needs.

Choose your niche carefully because everything you do going forward will depend on how well you understand the niche. Each of your videos must have intent and a purpose. The perfect niche should be something that your audience are already searching for. It should not be extremely competitive that you become a small fish swimming against the sharks. The perfect niche should allow you to express your knowledge and passion for the subject matter.

Niches also allow you to get so close to your audience. Therefore, as much as you want to learn more about them, they should also enjoy the same benefit. Customers want to know more about what you are about. They should feel confident in your brand, such that they subscribe to get quality content about things that matter to them.

Niche Selection

Before you get into the content business, you must figure out your niche. This is the first step towards YouTube success. Popular YouTube channels succeed because the audience gets the right content that meets their needs. The last thing you want to do is upload random videos and hope that things will work out. That's a waste of resources.

Most content creators already know what they want to do when they start uploading content to their channels. This is because they usually focus on things that they love, or something they already do, so it comes to them naturally. If you are a musician, for example, your channel will be about music, or you can create content around your favorite instrument.

Now let's say you have been thinking about content creation on YouTube because you read how much influencers are making and you are excited about the prospects. You have time and all the resources necessary to start a successful YouTube career, but the only thing missing is how to identify the perfect niche. How do you go about it? Here are three important pointers to guide you:

1. Research market demand

Come up with a list of subjects you can create content around, and check to see if there is sufficient demand for them. It would be pointless creating content for a dead-end concept. Do not create content for something no one is searching for. Being unique is great, but not all the time. If you want to make money from YouTube, your niche must be something people look for all the time.

You can use tools like Google AdWords Keyword Planner to research content in different niches and see how many hits they receive per month. You will also see the level of competition in the niches. Google Trends shows you how popular topics trend from time to time. From here, you can tell whether interest in the subject is seasonal or if the demand increases with time.

2. Subjects you are passionate about

Take a moment and think of things you are passionate about. There's a good chance other people are as passionate about the subject as you are, or even more excited than you are. Passion is important, not just when starting your YouTube channel, but in every other business. There are times when things go wrong in the business environment, and without passion, you cannot ride the tide and survive the tough times.

It is easier to create content around subjects you are passionate about. Your YouTube channel will be a forever thing, so you will be creating content regularly. There will be difficult moments when you feel frustrated, run out of ideas, or you just feel tired and fatigued. Your passion for the subject can uplift you during such moments.

When presenting content to your audience, they can tell how passionate you are about the subject from your excitement. This is the kind of genuineness that keeps customers coming back. If you are not passionate about the subject, your content might feel like chores, leaving everyone bored.

3. Study the competition

What's the nature of the competition in your selected niche? Competition comes into play in many ways. For example, how long will it take for your channel to get attention and recognition? The answer to this lies in the number of active YouTube users in that niche. If you love a subject but realize that the market is oversaturated, you will struggle to make an impact in that niche. That market has established leaders, and for a beginner, you might never make it.

Assuming that you don't have a specific topic in mind when you get on YouTube, you might be at an advantage because you have more room for experimenting. Search for a niche that has great demand but limited competition. However, if YouTube will be part of your marketing strategy, you should already have an idea of where to start. If you are in a segment whose niche is competitive, do not fret just yet. You can still make it by targeting keywords with low competition and working your way up. It will be hard work, might take longer to realize results, but it is not impossible.

Think about other YouTube content producers for example, how are they doing it? With all the competition in their niche, how do they hold the fort and keep going strong? Watching some of their videos, try and answer the following questions:

1. Why do people keep coming back to watch their videos all the time?
2. What type of content are they offering?
3. How is their content delivery?
4. What do they do to keep you engaged throughout?

Dive into the comments section and see what their audience is talking about. Are they angling for more insight or improvements? Put yourself in their position and try to resolve the audience's concerns. What can you add to the subject such that the audience would love the outcome? Can you present the same ideas from a different perspective? What can you do to give the audience a better value than they are currently getting?

Identifying a niche market can be difficult, but if you look in the right places, you can find everything you need. The secret is to try and find flaws within the market and offer solutions. Offer value in a qualitative manner, be authentic and unique and you will stand out from everyone else even in a saturated market.

Popular YouTube Niches

YouTube is a great place to be. People are making a living off the platform, and you should too. There are many niches, some more profitable than others. With millions of content to watch in different niches, you have so many options to work with. Everyone starts from somewhere, so come up with a strategy and trust the process. In this section, we will look at some of the top niches on YouTube, and hopefully, you can use this to kickstart your content career in the right direction.

1. Challenge videos

There's a trending challenge almost every other week on social media. Some of these challenges start from other social networks like TikTok or Instagram and become a hit on YouTube. Everyone seems to be creating a new challenge. If you are starting your YouTube career, this is a good place to start because you will get an instant audience and gain subscribers.

Challenge videos work because they tap into our innate desire to see other people make a fool of themselves. Besides, most of the challenges are hilarious and will trend beyond their expiry date as memes. With everyone joining the wave, you can ride the challenge wave and make your brand visible.

2. Vlogging

Would you like to share your life with the world? This is what vlogging is about. You can choose an aspect of your life and share it online. Vlogging is one part of YouTube responsible for incredible engagement numbers. You can vlog about anything. The age of reality TV is probably one of the reasons why vlogs became a hit.

Vlogging fills that voyeuristic need that makes us want to compare ourselves with other people. At times you are just curious to see what's going on in their lives.

Vlogging can be a big thing for you, especially if you surround yourself with supportive people who are as enthusiastic about your project as you are.

There are many vloggers on YouTube fitting every aspect of life. Content creators vlog about anything from vacationing to exotic destinations, to single life, food, and sports. Find your target audience, zero in on them, and feed their appetite. Focus on that category and grow the audience. If you want to know how big this market is, many vloggers eventually quit their day jobs to focus on their YouTube careers full time.

3. Gaming

If there's one market that is worth all the attention it gets, the gaming market is it. Gamers are a peculiar lot. Tapping into this market is amazing because gamers generally follow their content and content providers religiously. As soon as a new game is released gamers flock to YouTube and other gaming platforms to find out as much as they can about them.

Some games are incredibly difficult, and you might struggle to get through the missions. All you have to do is record your gameplay and tactics for beating such a level, upload it online and your audience will come through. Another way of going into this is by becoming a YouTube gamer. Before you venture into this field, however, you must invest in the right equipment. There is so much money in gaming, and you might even land yourself an endorsement.

4. Tech videos

The beauty of the tech industry is that new products are released all the time. Users need to know how to get the most value from these products, and this is where you come in. Cameras, tablets, phones, and wearables are a hit in this section. Search for your phone model on YouTube and you will find hundreds of videos exploring your device.

Seeing someone use a product you fancy gives you a different feel and can also help you preempt future challenges using that device. Most people run to YouTube as soon as they have a problem with their devices to see if theirs is an isolated case or a common problem. Others check YouTube reviews before they buy a new product. The information you gain from such channels gives you an upper hand when you go to the stores to buy something, or before you make an online purchase.

The tech video niche is amazing, and as much as there are many content producers in this field, you can always create a name for yourself. Besides, many viewers try to narrow down the content to their location because it gives them hope that you use similar devices. This is true considering that some manufacturers produce slightly different device variations for each region they cover.

5. Product reviews

Today many people buy products or subscribe to a service after watching a review online. While you can read the reviews, watching someone go through the processes gives you more confidence. You can follow their steps keenly and try to recreate their experience.

This creates a conversation point in case the outcome is not similar. Besides, product reviews can earn you free products and subscriptions from advertisers.

6. Tutorials

Tutorials have also become a hit, and the best thing about them is that you can create content in any field. Think of anything you are good at, you can create a tutorial out of it. Perhaps you are good at fixing motorbikes, makeup, hydroponic farming, you name it. People come to YouTube every day to learn and you will be amazed how much value this adds to their lives.

DIY enthusiasts, for example, are your biggest market for tutorials. You can watch a project or craft and with some practice, you will get better at it. You can even watch tutorials on how to create amazing content for your YouTube channel. The beauty of YouTube is that everyone can learn something from anyone. As long as you can do something confidently, there's always someone willing to learn from you.

7. Diet and weight loss

Weight loss, dieting, and healthy living are a promising place to start for a newbie. Before you start, you can watch a few videos in this niche to see how the top content providers are doing it. A good thing about this niche is that the market has a high demand for content. From fasting, vanish, exercise routines that work, successful diets, meal prep, there is so much content you can work on. You can even combine different concepts in one video to gain a wider reach.

Intermittent fasting, for example, trends from time to time. Time your content accordingly and you will hit the jackpot. You can time content around wedding season or the holidays. There's always someone looking to go the extra mile to improve their physique, metabolism, look better, get in shape, and so on.

8. Food reviews

Who doesn't love a good food review? We must eat, and for the same reason, food reviews will always have an audience. This is perhaps one of the most saturated niches in the game, so you must be careful about your approach. There are already industry leaders, but that does not mean you cannot make it.

Content creators in this niche often try new menus from different restaurants and grade them at the end of the video. You must, however, have your diet in check, and a solid workout plan because you will be eating a lot of food. Food reviews come in handy for people who want to try new dishes, or tourists who come to your area and are looking for fun things to do, or new restaurants to eat in the neighborhood.

9. Prank videos

Pranks get a lot of attention today, especially when a celebrity or any other popular person is the butt of the joke. Before you go into pranks, however, you must think it through and be ready to go the extra mile. It takes a lot to script a good one. Luckily, YouTube is full of prank videos, and if you run out of ideas, you can always watch some of them and come up with something solid for your brand.

Even if you borrow ideas from other pranks, your execution must be authentic. Give it a catchy title and ensure your video production quality is amazing. Pranks can get you attention easily because like challenges, many people enjoy it when you make a fool of someone.

Chapter 4:

Creating Unique and

Valuable Content

Content creation is an interesting industry. New creators join the fold every day while others quit. One of the reasons why some creators quit is because they don't feel they can meet the audience's expectations. Online audiences are drawn to a lot of things, but the most important is great content. Great content will build your brand. This is something that many video producers tend to overlook, hence their poor performance. The fact that you can shoot incredible videos using some of the best equipment in the industry will count for nothing if your content is terrible. People love stories, so your videos should be convincing.

Just like blog writing and other forms of written content, your video content must be amazing. You will get more exposure this way. You are after authentic, organic engagements, and to achieve that, you must provide your audience with quality content. Let's jump in and look at what it takes to create amazing content below:

1. Originality

There are many copycats in content creation, and most of them never make it. Online users today are keen on the kind of content they consume, and will easily call you out as a fraud when they realize you lack originality. Originality goes hand in hand with personality. You might upload a video on something that has been done many times before, but what sets you apart from everyone else is how you do it. Give it a personal touch.

While at it, there is only so much that you can do with a common subject. Try and dig deeper to find content that has not been overused before. Note that in content creation, you usually get feedback relevant to the kind of content you produce. It is easier to lose traction than gain it, so instead of focusing your energy on content that has been recycled many times, take more time to research and come up with something unique.

2. Catchy headlines

The catchy headline is the oldest trick in the book, and it works like a charm all the time. Everywhere you go, from newspapers to magazines online, headlines will always work. With audience time and viewership available at a premium, most people never go beyond headlines. Other than the witty headline, make sure your content lives up to expectations. Catchy headlines with terrible video content will get you bad reviews and attention.

3. Actionable content

What should your viewers do after watching your video? Depending on the kind of content you create, a call to action adds more insight. If yours is an entertainment channel, people should watch your videos, get entertained, and search for more of your content. If you produce educational content, they should feel they learned something useful and apply the skills in their lives. After watching your videos, the audience should feel they are better off than they were before they watched it. That is proof that your content adds value to their lives.

4. Offer solutions

We live in an age where people seek all kinds of answers online. This creates a good opportunity for you to provide feasible solutions. Think of Google and other search engines for a minute. People ask many questions every minute, and the search engine returns videos and links to possible solutions. In a few clicks, you find what you were looking for and you are satisfied.

This is the kind of impact your videos should provide audiences. When they watch your content, they should learn something that improves their lives. Say you upload makeup videos. At the end of your video, you should have answered some questions your viewers might have struggled with for a while. By offering solutions to problems, you position yourself as a go-to guide for something.

5. Credibility and accuracy

Believability is another factor you should never take for granted in content creation. Many people will watch your video, and some of them could be more knowledgeable about the subject than you are. For this reason, always ensure you check your facts before you post anything online. Of course, you might make a mistake here and there, and if that happens, follow it up with a retraction, explaining the new position.

As much as you are working towards engaging content, never forget that you are creating content for consumption by audiences who might check your facts. Your competitors might also be looking at your content and use your errors and mistakes to bring you down. Do not treat your content lightly. Content creation is hard work, and the best content takes a lot of time and resources to create. Give your audience the best content and they will show their appreciation in kind.

Creating the Buyer Persona

You need a content strategy going forward. A content strategy involves more than deciding the type of content you want to create. This is where the buyer persona comes in. The idea is to identify the audience, where to find them, and how to speak to them. People should watch your videos and feel like the message was directed to them. That personal touch creates a strong bond between the audience and your content.

When producing content, you should research deeper and find out important details that can help you get the message across to viewers better. Research about the fears, challenges, obstacles, and other things in the lives of your audience and use your content to provide answers and solutions. You might not always get everything right, but you should hit closer home. You are presenting content to humans, not bots, so your content should be positioned in a way that makes them feel connected, and appreciated.

It is impractical to create content that speaks to everyone who comes across your video. This is why a buyer persona is useful. The buyer persona is more or less a semi-fictional creation that represents your ideal audience. Who would benefit the most from your content and become loyal followers? Creating this persona involves a bit of guesswork and lots of research. From there, you will keep refining and tweaking the character traits to get the closest picture of the ideal person to benefit from your content.

To define this persona, start by looking at the demographics. Consider things like gender, age, job titles, and region. Most of this data is already available in the CRM you use. This is more or less about profiling your audience. Say your content is in the fitness niche, for example. You might have something like this:

> *Janet, a fitness instructor in her mid-thirties*
>
> *Her job involves running fitness classes, providing nutritional advice, advertising on social media, and lead generation.*

From this information, your buyer persona might include the following:

1. Female audience
2. Age group mid-20s to mid-30s

3. Fitness and nutrition

This gives you a starting point. You can update more information by thinking about Janet's needs. To be precise, you don't know Janet. You probably have never even met her, but with basic information about her, you can create a fictional person whose needs you will attend to in your videos. A simple online survey can give you more information about Janet and her needs. You might not know specifically what she needs, but having the slightest idea can make a big difference. For example, from polls and surveys, you might learn that she needs to grow her fitness practice by teaching people how to workout from the comfort of their homes, without purchasing equipment.

Further down the line, you will want to address the challenges she is facing. For example, most of her clients are frustrated by falling into a plateau stage soon after they start working out, and give up altogether. She needs a way to keep them motivated to see the results.

What you have done so far is build a blueprint of what the audience needs, from basic demographic information. You learn a lot from the challenges people face because this is what stops them from taking action and moving to the next stage. This is what a buyer persona does for your content. As you can see, it is fictional, but it attempts to answer questions about your audience, whose answers bring you closer to addressing their needs.

You cannot go through this process for each of your audiences. This is where tweaking comes in handy.

From Jane's basic profile, you can create a few more personas and sample the common traits that appear in each of them. Use the commonalities to build the ultimate persona. As you do that, remember that your audiences are human beings whose lives are more complicated than the persona you created. Many times their decisions will go against the grain, even if you develop the most elaborate persona. Do not panic when this happens.

Content Creation Tips

You can tell so much about a content creator from the techniques they apply in their work. Naturally, you want to put yourself in the best position in terms of audience engagement and producing amazing videos. To do this, you must have a good understanding of how people think and find meaning in their environments. Use this knowledge to show them your content sufficiently meets their needs.

A good video editor should be able to empathize. By empathy, you should cater to the needs of the audience. Anyone who watches your videos should resonate with your message such that they can suppose what your motivations for that recording were. So, how do you make the best content? The secret lies in your video editing skills, so let's look at some important tips to get you going:

1. **Camera angles**

You should try and get the best angles when shooting videos. As you record the footage, try to get a good balance between the attention your virtual audience gets, and the attention the speaker gets. Put yourself in the shoes of your audience and think of some of the things they would be looking for assuming they were in the room. You can work with an imaginary audience while recording the videos. This helps you choose the most practical camera angle to reconstruct every moment. Your aim should be choosing the best angles that allow you to convey your message to the audience without them being distracted.

2. Choose the appropriate shots

For beginners, most content creators cannot tell when to use wider, medium, or close-up shots. In practice, you should cut on different camera angles where necessary so that the audience can appreciate your background. To do this, you must use more close-up shots than medium or wide shots.

Close-up shots are amazing because they give your audience context. They keep them engaged and highlight subtle things like facial expressions and other gestures in the presentation. With such a view, it is easier for you to appeal to the audience. Note that body language is often embodied. You might not notice it yet, but viewers will often lose interest when they realize a disconnect between your body language and your speech pattern.

3. Capture the motion

Online audiences notoriously have a short attention span. You have a brief window of opportunity to capture their attention. An easy way of keeping them hooked is working with different camera angles. This is more interesting and adds a dynamic twist to your video than using one camera angle throughout the video.

4. Go easy on the graphics

When preparing the video, you probably have a script prepared. Your script can stay on the screen for a while as you try to figure out how to break the recordings into manageable sections. Ideally, you want to ensure the relevant parts of your recording show up in time to be in sync with your words. While working on this, be careful not to be overzealous with the graphics and lose the audience's attention.

5. Filter out the errors

From technical errors to speech errors, make sure you edit them all out. Once you record the video, take your time with the editing and iron out the errors. The last thing you want is your audience correcting your speech or pointing out errors instead of focusing on your message and delivery.

Following the points above, you can edit and deliver some amazing work. We have, however, just talked about editing your videos. This is assuming that you already have the content ready. Moving from idea to a concept is another challenge altogether. To bring your ideas to life, there are two important factors you must consider, having a solid plan and the audience journey. Let's look at these briefly:

1. Proper planning

You must have a solid plan. The idea alone might not count for much, but an execution strategy will make all the difference. What message do you wish to convey, how do you intend to deliver the message? You probably want to evoke some emotion in the audience. What response do you need from them if you trigger those emotions? These are some of the things that go into planning that you should think about. At the same time, plan for all the materials, tools, and equipment you might need.

2. Audience journey

How did the target audience arrive at this point? People love stories, and if they find something or someone whose tales they can resonate with, they feel their needs are taken care of. As you think of the stories you want to tell the audience, have you thought about their story? How does your content align with the audience's journey? If you can both end up on the same page, you will have struck the sweet spot in content creation and delivery. Your engagement metrics will be over the roof.

Working along the lines above, you should also find a voice that resonates with your audience. Don't make them feel like you are talking down on them. Your presentation should be clear, concise, and address the issues aptly. Be unique in your presentation, and try not to introduce too many ideas at the same time.

Generating Content Ideas

Brands and websites all over the world produce videos every day. Videos have become a valuable asset, especially for social networks, with their algorithms prioritizing video engagements. This is why videos should play an important role in your content strategy going forward. Most internet marketers and content creators agree that videos deliver the best return on investment compared to other kinds of content. All this is possible because of three reasons:

1. Videos are effective tools in building brand awareness
2. You get more conversions using video than any other type of content
3. Videos help you connect with customers because of their authenticity

These are not the only reasons why content creators prefer video, but they are the main ones. To realize these benefits you must learn how to find good ideas and work on them effectively. One of the biggest challenges you might experience is identifying the most effective material for your videos. Other than that, assuming you already know what to do, how do you get the technical details and the creative content in sync to produce the best content? Let's look at some of the top content types available on YouTube, and how to build great content around them:

1. **Live recordings**

There's currently a growing market of live streams, with content producers trying to outdo each other. Live content is amazing because of its raw nature. You can make it interactive, fun, and use any means possible to give the audience a glimpse into your brand or life. If you want to know how big live streams are, almost all social media platforms have a live feature.

Most online audiences today would rather watch a live recording than read a blog or article about something. With live recordings, there is so much you can present to your audience, including live training sessions, tours, product introductions, seminars, and webinars.

Given the potential for growth using live videos, how can you make sure your live stream will become a success? First, you must work together with your audience. Let them know in advance when you will be going live. It could be unfortunate, going live with no one expecting you online.

Internet connection is an important part of a successful stream. Ensure you have a strong and reliable connection before you go live. Nothing sucks like devoting your time to a live stream only to end up with a buffering stream throughout.

To build a loyal following, go online frequently and while at it, switch up the broadcast content to keep things interesting. As people join the stream, interact with them, and greet them. Mentioning someone's handle makes them feel special, so you should consider that too. At the end of the broadcast, you can give hints of what you will discuss in the next session to build anticipation.

2. Tutorial videos

Tutorials are a popular content type with many people looking for hands-on instructions to fix things or avoid spending on handymen and other technicians. If you have ever tried to follow instructions from a tutorial website without a video, you probably understand the challenges involved. A video tutorial is more practical than reading a printed set of instructions.

Let's say you bought a MacBook Pro and you want to glimpse under the hood and see how things work. It is easier to follow a video tutorial than to read how to open the machine. Video tutorials don't just tell you what to do, they show you. There's so much content you can choose from, you must be original in your approach. Another reason why tutorial videos are such a hit is that they help you create value for the audience by showcasing your expertise in some skill.

It takes some work to make a great tutorial video. First, ensure you prepare the script in detail and rehearse the presentation effectively. Other than presenting the video, highlight the purpose of the video and present it without losing track. Finally, make the tutorial personal and genuine. Your personality should shine through.

3. Exclusive videos

Curiosity is not just a cat thing, we go through the same thing too. It is in our nature to want to know why things work the way they do. You get so much satisfaction when you know how something works, instead of believing in the magic of its existence. This allows you to create amazing content behind the scenes. With exclusive content, you can show viewers how things work. It doesn't have to be something fancy, at times all you need is to show the team behind your amazing videos. Capture the moments, the unedited content, the blips, mishaps, and errors.

Everyone is probably used to seeing the refined quality content you post online. It comes as a surprise, therefore, when you take them behind the scenes and show them your production team in their element. It almost feels like watching an animal in its natural habitat. Going behind the scenes gives your viewers an authentic concept. They see themselves in your flaws and mistakes, and your brand becomes relatable. This approach can help you build trust by humanizing your content, team, brand, company, and highlighting the creative geniuses behind your brand.

The secret to creating amazing exclusive videos is to try and create that human connection. While shooting such content, focus the attention on anyone but yourself, which could be your audience, customers, or team. At the end of the recording, you can request ideas from your audience feedback, or promote your products.

4. Explainer videos

Almost similar to exclusive videos described above, you can use explainer videos to show people what your product or service does. If you solve some problem for the audience, use the video to explain to them how you do it. Using such videos, you can also show the audience how you deliver value, and more importantly, why paying for your goods or services will be worth their while.

People are generally more inclined to purchase something after watching a video of it than reading about it. This is where explainer videos come in handy. You don't have to go overboard with the video either. It should be a brief video that answers important questions customers might have about your brand.

How do you make a compelling explainer video? The first rule is to make it short, simple, and succinct. The video must only address one message, within 60-90 seconds. To get it right, write down the script and practice it. Your goal is to convince the audience in that short duration.

Research some of the challenges that viewers have and explain how your product or service solves that problem. Other than that, explain how your product or service works, and round off your explainer video with a call to action.

Engaging content can help you strengthen your brand and marketing strategy. You don't need to hire a team of experts to handle it for you. For a start, even a smartphone can do the work. Away from the technical aspects, let your charisma shine through the video, focus on delivering the content message in a way that the audience will appreciate. If you implement your content strategy correctly, your videos can help you create or increase awareness of your brand, connect with more customers, and convert sales into leads.

Overcoming Creators' Block

Creatives usually go through a difficult plateau phase where it feels like the creative juices run out. Everything else comes to a standstill, you become lethargic and can barely come up with fresh ideas. It gets worse when everything else seems to be on a go-slow. You wake up one day and realize your subscribers are not growing, the page views, the number of visitors, and even your income have stagnated. This period is frustrating, and you might even consider giving up on your project altogether. You have probably heard of writers' block for bloggers and content writers. The same concept applies to video creation too, and no one is immune to it. Let's look at some things you can do to get you out of that muddle when you get to that point:

1. Shelve results and focus on actions

Like most content creators, you might fall for the allure of results. Granted, everyone wants to see results. You work hard on your channel and need to see the numbers making sense. You might also be looking at the monetization angle and for that, you must see results. In your content strategy, you are probably thinking about the number of visitors you should get every month and how much money your channel should make, and this boxes you into a corner.

These goals are realistic and they keep you motivated to achieve results. However, they do not show what you should do to get there. That is where you get stuck in the plateau phase. Instead of dwelling on the results, shift your attention to the things you must do to achieve them. For example, come up with a list of 15 content ideas and choose the top 5.

While the results matter, dwelling on them so much can get you stuck in the plateau phase for a while. Be proactive when you get to this stage and think in terms of what you can do to get things moving.

2. Consistent effort

The average content creator will lose interest when they encounter creators' block. From a lack of interest, you might not see the need to work hard, after all, the numbers are not growing. Before you know it, your form dips, and poor results become the order of the day. This is a difficult period, but you must be consistent in your effort.

Keep pushing forward. It might not seem like things are changing, but subtle consistent efforts eventually yield results. Do not be cowed by the stalled growth. It is a phase, and it comes to an end at some point. By the time the phase times out, the small steps you made will make a difference.

3. Brainstorm

Your creativity dips in the plateau phase so much that you might not feel confident enough to produce quality content. At this point, you might also lose the plot and stop focusing on what works for your audience. Shifting your attention to what works for you instead of the audience is a bad move that might cost you in the long run.

You can get out of this phase by brainstorming. Discuss your ideas with someone so that they can help you stay on course. You still need to get visitors, traffic, and organic leads from your content. Brainstorming can help you feel rejuvenated. Creatives struggle through this a lot, so do not feel different when things are not going your way.

There are many ways of brainstorming, and all the ideas don't have to be productive either. Just talk to someone and write down things like challenges your readers face, the industry trends, controversial topics, predictions, anything that comes to mind. Get into a free-flow mode and don't judge yourself or your ideas. Eventually, you will end up with a long list of ideas that might be useful even after you get out of the plateau phase.

4. Networking

This might be a good time for you to up your networking efforts. The beauty of content creation is that you are constantly surrounded by a network of brilliant minds. If you feel stuck, dive into your network and talk to people about your struggles. You might even start a new network in the process. Note that a strong network will not necessarily fill your wells with content ideas, but it can help you meet influential people in your niche.

Do not be afraid to reach out to someone you would like to know in your industry, even if they seem light years ahead of you. Reaching out can be as simple as introducing yourself and talking about something you are working on. The bottom line is that everyone gets to that point in life where ideas dry up, and they feel less enthusiastic about working on anything. Don't let his blip derail your entire plan.

Chapter 5:

Attracting and Growing

Your Audience

YouTube is a powerhouse in the content realm, and this is one of the reasons why you should put a lot of work into getting subscribers to your channel. The network is brimming with an audience yearning for quality content, and if you can provide it, you will have the most amazing experience on social media ever. YouTube is full of opportunities for content creators and marketers, but most of them lose the plot because they don't know how to promote their content properly and impress their audiences. Considering the number of users on the platform, we will discuss a few steps you can use to gain more subscribers to your channel. Most of the time your channel could be struggling, not because you don't know what to do, but how to do it right. Let's look at some simple methods you can use to attract more users below:

1. Understand the technical aspects

One of the reasons why many YouTube channels struggle is because of something as simple as the thumbnail. Many content creators do not think much about this at all. You want to make sure your website gets the attention it deserves. The thumbnail might be such a small thing it could even be insignificant, but it makes a big difference for your channel.

It takes a split second for someone to decide what they are watching on your channel. The difference between staying and moving along comes down to the thumbnails. Each time you upload a video, spare a few minutes and choose the right thumbnail that works for it. This is one of the technical aspects of growing a YouTube that most content creators take for granted.

Another technical issue you should look into is how to work with end cards. People generally like to associate with success. If they see your channel is growing, they would want to be a part of that success. This is where end cards come in handy. A visible subscribe button nudges, viewers, to subscribe to your channel. They enjoy the content and wish to keep getting the good stuff.

You might also want to look into embedded videos. Embedding allows you to share your content widely. Instead of coming to YouTube for your videos, people can watch them wherever they are embedded. The good thing about this is that it reduces the risk of losing your audience to competitors or other unrelated videos. Remember we mentioned earlier that YouTube is inherently designed to keep viewers on the platform. YouTube recommends similar content to ensure the viewers stay hooked. Through embedded videos, your viewers can enjoy your content without distractions.

2. Predictions and riding trends

An important skill most content creators lack is the ability to predict or preempt trends. You don't necessarily have to be the genius that starts a trending topic online, but you should learn how to ride trends for your benefit. If you notice your engagement and views are dropping, you can use the numbers behind a trending topic to see how things will work for you. An important point to note when chasing trends is to learn how to identify whether the trend will work for you or not. Trends can be an easy way of luring viewers back to your channel if you ride them well.

3. Work with influencers

Influencer marketing is an important procedure many content creators are using to grow their channels and presence online. Influencer marketing is great for your business for many reasons. First, you leverage your content against an individual that already has a huge audience and a religious following.

Influencer marketing works well for you because your content benefits from the exposure of the influencer's channel and networks. This could also introduce your content to a different niche, market, or audience. While that works, you should also ensure you align yourself with influencers who share a similar growth mindset, and objectives as you do.

Influencer marketing works, but content creators fail at it because they choose the wrong influencers. The numbers might be pretty, but don't be fooled just yet. Look at influencers who do not just have the numbers, but the engagement too. The benefit of this is that you enjoy steady subscriber growth because of access to an audience that already knows what it wants, and where to find it.

Irrespective of your niche or industry, you will never run short of vloggers and other content creators willing to share your content. It's a win-win for them too, because they also get exposure to your existing audience. Piggybacking on someone's fame and authority can help you with steady audience growth. This is an opportunity you should not let pass you by.

4. Promoting your videos

People are more likely to subscribe to your channel when they watch more of your videos. The challenge is how to get someone so hooked they can watch more than two videos in one sitting. The secret is to promote your videos in the end screen. How do you do this? When producing videos, allow an extra ten seconds at the end for this. With YouTube's end screen editor, you can insert a link to one of your related videos. This works well because when someone watches your video and they see a link to the related video, it makes them want to check it out.

These procedures are simple, yet many content creators never get it right. You don't have to buy subscribers like most channels do today. Make these simple steps part of your growth strategy and you will be on the right path.

Promoting Your Channel

YouTube has an active market of billions of users signing in to the platform every month. For a content creator, this is paradise. Unfortunately, most content creators lack the skills to tap into this market. With billions of users on the platform, billions of content are similarly produced to feed this audience. If you don't position your content properly, you risk losing yourself in the sea of content.

There's a technical bit of YouTube that most content creators never realize - the YouTube algorithms and their impact on your channel performance. The algorithms count for most of what people watch on YouTube, up to as much as 70%. Your struggle, therefore, is to find a delicate balance between positioning your content for the algorithms and for your audience. Clicks on your video are no longer the only thing needed to estimate performance. YouTube currently emphasizes a mix of user satisfaction and engagement. For this, the following factors come into play:

1. Session time - the overall time viewers spend on YouTube
2. Watch time - how long viewers watch your video

YouTube algorithms are written to give prominence to audience interaction. The emphasis is on audience retention and long-term user engagement. Expert content creators find ways around the YouTube algorithms, which might be costly for someone who is starting out. To get you out of that meddle, the following are some simple tactics you can use:

1. Channel collaborations

Did you know you can get support from other channels whose audiences are alien to you? Cross-promotion is one way content creators support one another. It is also a good way to grow your audience so fast. The concept of cross-promotion is simple, one content creator shares your content with their audience. As much as you are new to that audience, the content creator sharing your work almost instantly gives you validation with their audience.

Because of the authority they have with their audience, they are persuaded to have a look at your work. Cross-promotion seems simple, but there are two factors you must look into. Look for content creators whose dynamics are similar to yours in terms of the audience type and their influence level.

In terms of the audience type, you can look at the comments section to learn more about your audience and their interests. Based on this information, you can easily find exciting content creators for cross-promotion.

Considering the level of influence, you must offer something in return for your co-content creator. When someone looks at your audience, they should hope to gain as much as you will gain from their audience. For example, you have a higher chance of partnering with a content creator whose channel has roughly the same number of subscribers as you do. If the content creator's numbers are five times more than yours, for example, cross-promotion becomes a challenge because it's highly likely they don't feel your subscribers can add them any value. You can use tools like Social Blade to identify channels that share similar metrics as yours.

2. Ask viewers for help

There's nothing wrong with asking your viewers for help. Compared to other social media networks, you will realize that the YouTube audience is generally better receptive to a call to action than audiences in other social networks. People like content, comment, and subscribe so easily on YouTube, and you can work this to your advantage. You can ask for help in any of the following three ways:

First, at the beginning of your video, you can encourage users to hit the subscribe button so they can receive timely updates from your channel. Secondly, you can take a shot at the description. This is a 50/50 chance because while it works for optimization, most YouTube users barely read the description. There is no harm, however, in asking viewers to share your content in the description.

Finally, you can use end screens. Naturally, people expect some request or call to action at the end of your video. You can ride this expectation and ask viewers to share your content. If you use this approach, be careful not to change frames dramatically. The secret is to maintain the speech pace and keep talking until the end screen shows up. Try not to include a long pause between the end of your content and the end screen.

3. External social media promotion

If you have other social media platforms, you can use them to promote your YouTube content. Even if you only have a handful of friends and followers, you can still generate traction for your content. To make this work best for you, try and engage this circle as soon as you release new content on YouTube. Sharing content too long after you released it on YouTube might appear like it is a last-resort act of desperation, and your circle might feel you only come to them when you need them.

Thinking long-term, you can also research and reach out to websites whose embedded video content is similar to yours. Even those that don't have videos, you can reach out to them and inform them that their content resonates with your videos, and talk to them about using your video as media content. While this gives you more exposure, the benefit for them is that they get users to spend more time on their website, watching your video.

4. YouTube Stories

YouTube stories and the community tab are valuable resources you can use to push your agenda further. The idea behind these tools is to ensure that YouTube users get the full social media experience. Assuming that you have the community tab enabled in your channel, you can use this to ask the audience questions, driving engagement and interactions in the process. This is also a good place for you to introduce your upcoming content to the audience, building hype while at it.

YouTube stories is a concept that was popularized by social networks like Instagram. The difference is that while stories only run for 24 hours on Instagram, YouTube keeps them for 7 days.

5. Google traffic

Imagine getting a steady stream of traffic from Google, wouldn't that be amazing? Many content creators limit themselves to YouTube and rarely push their content outside of this platform. In the past, Google has become a reliable source of traffic. You should tap into this. Besides, YouTube is part of the Google bundle, so it is only fair that you seek traffic from Google.

Here's how it works - Google favors mixed content for some keywords, especially video. All you have to do is create a video snippet and a matching thumbnail, which the Google algorithms will use to send traffic your way.

6. Giveaways and contests

Contests and giveaways are great for community mobilization. They also help you create more activity on your channel. Let's face it, the online community is full of people seeking freebies. Tap into this and expand your horizons to a new audience by asking the participants to share their contest entries with their personal networks, get more likes, and hope to win something in the end.

Assuming you initially planned to award only the winner, you can rethink the rewards depending on the number of entries. If you receive more entries than you anticipated, you can award the winner and create additional awards for some of the top participants. This endears you to the audience because they realize that you appreciate their input. If you don't have products to give participants, you can talk to a brand to sponsor your contests.

Keeping Subscribers Engaged

You work so hard to create amazing content and are finally getting the subscribers. Seeing the number of subscribers increase on your channel is incredible. It shows progress and is proof that you are doing the right thing. If you thought getting subscribers was difficult, keeping them is even harder. This is because you don't just need the numbers, you want them actively engaging your content from time to time.

You have to set yourself apart from everyone else in your niche. Creating the YouTube channel, uploading videos, creating playlists, working on your logo, header and graphics, and filling in lots of information about your videos and channels is a lot of work, but it pays off in the long run if you do it well. Strive to make your channel unique, special, so that each time someone is on your channel, they feel something different. This is how you will keep subscribers around, and engaged.

Let's have a look at some simple things you can do to achieve this:

1. Help them find you

First, help more users find your channel. Creating amazing content that no one can find would be fruitless. YouTube is like a forest, and your channel might just be another tree in the forest. If your tree fell and no one heard it fall, no one would know about it. Create a buzz around your channel so that people are interested even if you are only making small waves.

Before people visit your channel, they need to know it exists. The easiest way of doing this working to bring your content to search results on YouTube and Google. To achieve this, you must learn to use creative keywords that will bring more users to your content instead of rivals' content. As more people share, comment on, and watch and like your video, the search engine algorithms assume our content and channel is important, and you get better rankings for relevant search keywords.

Use your current subscribers to gain more subscribers. If you engage them properly, they can become subtle brand ambassadors for your channel. One way of achieving this is through social media. Prepare them for content you are yet to release. Remember how movies create a buzz around upcoming releases? Do the same thing. Some users prefer to use the Browse Channels feature on YouTube to see what your channel is about. This is where first impressions matter. The more appealing your channel looks to them, the more likely the audience will spend more time on it.

2. Building relationships

Engagements are built on relationships. When viewers feel they find value in your content, they stay on much longer and share your content with other people in their networks. From a content creator's perspective, you creating good relationships with your audience will help you build a community around your content. For this to materialize, communicate with your audience frequently.

Once they subscribe to your channel, follow them keenly in the comments section and engage them. Discuss their views, take them into consideration, and address them directly when responding to their requests. Use this chance to introduce them to some of your other social media handles to engage them further.

The comments section is a good place to create all kinds of relationships. You will find users who follow you on all your social media accounts just so that they never miss out on anything.

3. Channel description

A clear channel description also makes it easier for viewers to find and engage with your content. Through the description, they know more about your channel before they watch any of your videos. If they are impressed by the description and it aligns with their interests, there is a higher chance they will visit, subscribe, and share your content with their peers.

This is how easy it is to use your current subscribers to attract more. Anyone who likes your content will probably come back for more. Those who love the content, on the other hand, will subscribe. Think about this like a subscription magazine. If you reach out for your favorite magazine each time you see it, you will eventually subscribe and enjoy the convenience of receiving it in your inbox immediately when the new release is out.

YouTube subscriptions work in the same way. Channel viewers get the same option. Once they subscribe, the challenge you have is how to keep them hooked. All you have to do is make the subscription worth their while, or you risk losing them as fast as they came on board. Let's briefly look at simple things you can do to engage your subscribers below:

1.   Upload content frequently

Think of your channel as a TV station. Wouldn't it feel weird if each time you switched on to your favorite channel, you found the same content? If TV producers do not add new, fresh content all the time, even the most loyal viewers would quit. The same applies to your YouTube channel. If you are not adding content from time to time, you risk losing some of your subscribers.

The takeaway here is for you to have a vision for your channel. Even if you started this as a hobby, think long-term, and have a growth strategy. Think of yourself as a TV station and put in the work. You are no longer doing this for personal reasons, you have an audience, and their needs must be met.

2. Keep in touch

One of the most effective strategies for growing your subscriber base is to keep in touch with them. This is something many content creators take for granted because it feels like too much work. Granted, keeping in touch with subscribers can be a lot of work, but the payoffs are amazing in the long run.

YouTube statistics reveal that millions of users subscribe to channels every day. This is such a huge number to try and stay in touch with, but you can carve out a smart way to go about it. You don't have to talk to each of them, just share and encourage them to follow your social media accounts. It is easier to reply to messages and posts on social platforms like Twitter than in the comments section on your YouTube videos.

Besides, interacting with your audience on other social media platforms can give them a better view of your life away from the YouTube channel. For some viewers, seeing you in a different life makes your brand more relatable because they can put a face to it.

3. Use tagging to your advantage

Tags are an easy way of making your videos easy to find. When using tags, you essentially assign unique categories to the uploaded content such that it is easier to identify it, not just for your audience, but for the YouTube algorithms too. Content that is easy to find increases the chances of people seeing it, further increasing the odds of getting new subscribers.

If you follow the steps outlined above correctly, the next step for you will be establishing your channel as a brand. Brands make it easier for your audience to identify with your content. Let's explain this with an example. Imagine a brand like Adidas. If they changed their logo or slogan all the time, people would struggle to keep up. In the long run, the changes erode consumer confidence and most people would begin to wonder whether they have a genuine product or knock-offs.

Branding your channel and content is one way of establishing or restoring confidence in your products. Seeing the same Adidas logo and slogan for years is one of the reasons why many people stay on board. There are other brands out there that they can consider, but once they get hooked on Adidas, nothing else matters. Of course, Adidas has to go the extra mile and provide incredible product quality and services to meet consumer expectations.

Now, think of your channel in the same light. You should have your brand image figured out from the beginning. There is so much content online, similar or otherwise. You are probably venturing into a niche that already has established leaders. Branding your YouTube channel from the beginning gives your content identity. Your viewers know what your content is about from the start. They know who you are and this makes them confident in your brand. Apart from that, establishing a brand from the start shows the audience that you will be around for a long time.

Let's round off this section with some actionable tips on how to create that perfect brand on YouTube. The following five points will do the trick:

1. Channel header

When you sign in to your YouTube channel, you meet an empty banner. Next to it, there's an *Add channel art* button. Choose an image that is compelling and can sell your brand to the audience. Other than the image, you can add some good graphics that include your channel name.

Take things a notch higher and include your contact information in the channel header. This is where you include your names on other social media platforms. You can also mention how often you upload content on your channel. This way, immediately someone lands on your YouTube channel, they have all the information they need at a glance.

2. Brief introduction

Did you know you can market your content within your channel? Create a short video that runs before each video. You can make it three to five seconds long and insert it at the beginning of each video you upload. This short introduction becomes the label for all your content. Want to know how this works? Think of the number of times you watch movies, and look forward to seeing the roaring MGM lion or the torch-bearing lady from Columbia Pictures. You get used to such introductions that you instantly have high expectations of the movie.

The introduction creates a perception in the minds of your viewers that lasts forever. Be creative if you decide to use this option and make it compelling. You will love the outcome.

3. Channel trailer

The trailer plays automatically on your YouTube channel as long as someone is on it. The trailer can be a good way of advertising your content and channel. Create a video that gives the best representation of your brand. This can be a short clip informing the audience of how they can benefit from your content or channel. The clip should be the best advertisement for your brand.

4. Create playlists

How many videos have you uploaded on your channel? With lots of videos, you can create a playlist. You can organize your video playlists based on themes, content message, or whichever running order. Playlists are a good idea, but you must do it right. With the right concept, they can tell a story of your content and channel. If you do it wrong, you can end up confusing your audience.

5. Brand logo

The fact that companies spend millions on branding and logo design should tell you how important this is for your channel. Of course, you might not have the millions yet, but you can start thinking of the logo. Logo design on its own, might not be so expensive. However, the cost goes up when the companies have to track old logos and delete them from all available spaces. These are unnecessary costs you should not have to incur.

An easier way of going about the logo design and to avoid unnecessary expenditure in the future is to have a simple logo that encompasses everything your brand is about. A simple option is your name and image. Even if you change the brand logo some years into the future, as long as you still own the channel, you would not have to do so much about the redesign.

Branding your YouTube channel can be so easy, especially if you get everything right from the start. Without a proper strategy at the beginning, there will always be a risk of spending more in the future to rebrand. Take your time and give your channel the best start.

Chapter 6:

Measuring Performance

You have invested so much in your content strategy. Think of the effort, creativity, time, and other resources that went into creating and building your YouTube channel. After all the input, you need to know how your channel is performing. The information you get from your channel not only informs you about your performance, but also gives you insight on how to improve your content.

From the very beginning, you should learn how to track YouTube analytics, and build it into your marketing strategy. We will discuss some of the metrics you should look at, and how to use the results for growth. Understanding YouTube analytics is important if you are to get the most out of your channel. Each video performance and engagement is different from the next.

YouTube analytics allows you to quantify and compare the performance of each video. In the process, you can identify success and failure. The reports give you insight into opportunities for growth, and how to add value to your subscribers. You will then use that information to boost engagement and expand the reach of your brand online. Here are some of the key metrics that help you estimate your content performance on YouTube:

Watch Time

One of the first things everyone notices when they load a YouTube video is the number of views. People even boast how many views their videos receive over a short duration. You can understand the craze about views because they are an important metric in determining performance, and monetizing your content.

As impressive as the number of views is, on their own they cannot tell you much about your content or what to improve. Besides, looking at the influx of clickbait online, YouTube does not put so much weight on views either. You must put the views into context to get more value from them. For this reason, the YouTube algorithm considers views together with the watch time.

The watch time estimates the duration spent watching a video. Views count as soon as someone loads the video. If you look at the analytics dashboard and notice that your watch time is low, it means that while people might be loading your content, it is not engaging enough to keep them watching. This explains why raw views do not tell much about your content.

Some of the reasons why people might not be enjoying your content include poor video editing skills, dull content, or anything else that makes the audience feel disconnected from your content. Switch things up a bit. Try using a different video editing program, rethink your script, change the shooting location or settings, and so on. Do whatever you can to improve the overall output, and you might just see your engagements changing.

Raw views and the watch time are useful indicators of performance, but they can offer so much insight on their own. We will discuss other metrics and data that you will use alongside views and watch time to learn and improve the content and discoverability of your videos.

Real-Time Report

The number of views on your video will fall from time to time. This happens because YouTube analyzes the views to remove low-quality views and spam from the total. You will notice a two-day disparity between the public views on your videos and the information shown in your dashboard. You need the real-time report to estimate and measure your video reach as early as possible. From this report, you can see the number of views over the last 60 minutes, or even 48 hours. You can narrow down the views from specific videos or the entire channel.

Keeping an eye on the real-time report, you should investigate anomalies. For example, a sudden spike in views might mean that someone just shared your video on a different platform or social network. Such are good moments for jumping on the hype and boosting engagement. If someone shares your videos on Twitter, for example, you can use that moment to create or continue conversations on it and make the most of that moment before the traction cools down.

Knowing your performance in real-time is one of the reasons why this is an important metric. Besides, you can instantly find out where your content has been shared away from YouTube resulting in the spike, using the following search query:

YouTube ID -site:youtube.com (e.g. ImRJ76klNTc - site:youtube.com)

Once you identify the location, follow the conversation and contribute to it. This is all about building engagements.

Sources of Traffic

Where are your viewers coming from? This is a critical question whose answer helps you understand the content reach. In the analytics channel, go to the Traffic Sources page to see where all your traffic comes from. This panel also includes the viewer aggregate from each location. From this point, you will learn how your audience is finding your content. Traffic source is important because it helps you evaluate the quality of traffic. From this report, you can easily tell the most useful traffic, either specific to a given video or all across the channel.

The lesson you learn by studying traffic is that not all sources provide quality. For example, let's say you get more traffic from YouTube search than any other source. Using this information, think of how to optimize content and your videos so that they show up frequently, not just in the common searches, but also for most of the keywords people use to find your videos.

Demographics

The general statistics about your audience will not tell you so much about them. To improve your videos and engagement, you must go deeper and understand what constitutes your audience. The demographics section in YouTube analytics will give you more information about your audience, including the following:

1. Location
2. Gender
3. Age
4. Devices they use

If you post product videos, you might notice you reach some customers that you normally would not access using normal search engines. Many content creators look at age and gender and use this information to inform future targeted campaigns.

Still on the demographics page, click on *More* and select *Geography*. This shows you where your viewers come from. Most brands don't care so much about the location because as long as they get the views, they are satisfied. This changes if you are merchandising. From the location, you can think of targeted ads, or even explore the opportunity and consider the logistics of launching in the new market.

Go further into the statistics and narrow down on each country. This gives you a breakdown of the gender and age graph for each country. This is useful information to create videos targeting each region in response to geographic trends.

Playback locations

This answers the question "*how are people discovering my videos?*" Playback locations helps you understand whether your content is discoverable through external websites or just within YouTube. From this page, you can see the views in terms of where your audience plays the video. The options include mobile devices, embedded videos, YouTube watch page, and YouTube channel page.

Investigate each of the locations to see where your content is most popular. The lesson here is whether your content is more popular on YouTube or outside on blogs and websites and using that information to optimize content.

Audience Retention

You can only get quality views from great content. On the audience retention page, you can tell how many times people stopped watching the video and at what point. This can help you figure out where you lose their attention or the reasons why they suddenly stop watching, and use this information to prevent such problems in the future.

The video duration also plays an important role in retention. For short videos, people generally watch all or most of the video. The retention statistics might be great by YouTube standards. However as your video length grows longer, the retention will probably drop.

There are two events in this report that you should be keen on:

1. Absolute audience retention

This shows you specific sections in your video that audiences enjoy by expressing the number of views for that section as a percentage of the total number of views your video gains. From this information, you can spot peculiar viewer behaviors like those who skip forward and ignore the opening tune and introduction credits.

2. Relative audience retention

This report is more or less a comparative competitor analysis. It compares your video against other content on YouTube of the same length to determine your performance in terms of keeping the audience's attention through the video.

This comparison is not as useful as the absolute audience retention because it only compares the video duration. Without factoring in the content, the results cannot add much value beyond the generalized comparison.

If you can identify a specific point in the video where you lose the audience, you can go back to the drawing board and find out the message or content at that point that is so negative that people stop watching your video.

This report only gives you analytics for one video at a time. You cannot, therefore, see the performance of your channel in general. To improve your overall performance, inspect a few other videos to identify unique behavior patterns and do something about it. You can rewrite the script or change the video format.

The highest drop-off rate for videos is usually in the first 15 seconds. Introductions make or break your video. This is where you lock the audience in or lose them, so if you realize a high drop-off rate, you can change this by shortening or removing the introduction, going right into the topic, or even changing the description and thumbnail to represent your idea clearly.

Subscriptions

Your subscribers might be current or potential customers interested in your niche content or products. This is why you should check how the numbers fluctuate. Are you gaining or losing subscribers? If you notice a sudden change in subscription, investigate and find out what event happened that led to that change.

Subscribers can also help you understand the global content reach better than a single video. You can, however, monitor how many subscribers you gain or lose after uploading a new video. Subscriptions are about exposure. More active subscribers mean more exposure for your content, and hopefully, better engagement.

Let's say from your content, you expect your target audience to be men between the ages of 18 and 25, but from your demographics page, you realize that there are older females in your channel who are active and the engagement is off the roof. You cannot ignore this. Instead, you can adjust the tone of your content in a way that also addresses the needs of the new audience cluster. At the same time, you can also rethink your content strategy so that you can directly win the attention of your intended demographic. Meeting the needs of your audience is mandatory if you are to get more subscribers.

You can attract more subscribers with each uploaded video by adding a call to action in the pitch. Encourage them to subscribe to your channel for more videos, insight, and anything else you offer that interests them.

Apart from the number of subscribers, another important metric you can look at is the subscriber rate. This is arrived at by dividing the total number of views by your net subscriber gain. Compare the performance of your videos, and commit more resources to promoting those videos that performed well in terms of gaining new subscribers.

Social Media Integration

Even if your content is already performing well on YouTube, you cannot ignore other social networks. Integrating other social media platforms into your content strategy is an important aspect of promoting content online. Bearing this in mind, find out who shares your content, and how they share it.

Under YouTube analytics, the sharing page shows the number of times your videos were shared on social networks outside YouTube. Where do most of your audience share your content? Say most of the shares are on Twitter. Come up with a social media strategy for Twitter to encourage and boost the effectiveness of this experience. Follow some of the users on their Twitter handles and engage them by liking or retweeting their posts relevant to your video or content.

Comments Section

The comments section is a good place to evaluate audience engagement. Look at the frequent commenters, their concerns, grievances, and anything else they draw your attention to. From the comments section, you can easily transform some of the viewers into customers and increase your content engagement.

Useful insight in the comments section include the date, frequency, and number of comments on each video. This information on your analytics dashboard can help you identify and act on opportunities as they present themselves. Going through the comments, you will find opportunities to promote products or services you sell, answer questions, and clarify ambiguities customers might have, or redirect customers to other resources and content you created.

The comments section is not just an avenue for your fans and followers, it is also a good place to position your brand as an engaging and approachable one. Positive and encouraging responses in your video give customers a good feeling about you, which is a good indicator for your brand.

Likes and Dislikes

The likes and dislikes page gives you the reaction and feedback from viewers about your content. Everyone is fascinated by likes. Dislikes, on the other hand, are often frowned upon. It is good practice not to ignore the dislikes. You certainly want to reduce the number of dislikes, so if you realize you are getting more dislikes over time, try and find out why this is happening. The comments section can reveal a lot about this.

Do not look at the dislikes in isolation. It's more practical to compare them against the number of likes your videos receive. If the dislikes keep rising, it's time to rethink your approach. For example, check the video title against the content to see if it lived up to expectations. You might be getting more dislikes because you are targeting the wrong audience, and they cannot relate to your message.

At times the dislikes might simply mean people do not agree with your message. In such cases, some people might express their contrary views in the comments. Perhaps the negative reception is because of poor production or your narration skills.

For whichever reason, dislikes might be frowned upon but if you investigate keenly, you can learn a lot from them, and improve your content for better performance and engagement in the future.

The YouTube analytics dashboard provides insight into your content and channel performance, but it is not the only platform. There are other applications and tools that you can use to get you similar information too. Social Blade is one such application that helps you compare your performance with competitors, role models, and partners in your niche.

With all the tools at your disposal, you should be able to understand your content performance, draw comparisons, and gain credible insight to help you refine your videos and channel in general for better engagement.

Devices

You might also want to know the kind of devices that people are using to access your channel. Under this tab, you will see the percentage of users accessing your videos on a games console, smart TV, tablet, mobile phone, or desktop computer. Why is this information important? The type of devices that people use often influence the kind of content they watch online, and their engagement level in general.

There's a higher chance of a desktop user to watch a video and purchase something online compared to a mobile user. Mobile users usually watch videos on the go, and will easily move on to something else after watching your video. If you want to drive conversations or engagement, this information will help you create an effective strategy.

The most practical approach would be finding a balance because you cannot restrict people on the kind of devices they use when watching content. For example, a few years ago the smartphone market was the fastest growing for YouTube content creators. While the market is still growing, there's more room for growth in the smart TV sector which is currently the fastest-growing market. As more people purchase smart TVs and replace their old ones, this is one area you need to think about when creating content, and how to convert the views to leads.

Revenue reports

Since you hope to earn from your YouTube channel, your attention must be drawn to the revenue reports section. It shows how much you earn on YouTube over a specific period. You can also track all your revenue streams from here. You will see the following:

1. Ads that are displayed on your videos, but are paid by other advertisers
2. Your paid ads on YouTube
3. Income earned from other platforms on YouTube

There are two important revenue stats you should track: the estimated revenue and estimated ad revenue. The estimated revenue is the expected income you will earn from any ads sold by Google. The estimated ad revenue is the expected income you will earn from DoubleClick and AdSense ads only.

You can filter these reports by location or dates to get more insight into your financial performance. Try and identify earning patterns or trends in the revenue reports. If you realize you earn more on specific days of the week, investigate and find out what makes those days different from the other days. Other than that, you can also modify your release schedule to upload content on a schedule that allows you to exploit such earning trends.

Another trick is to zoom out of the reports and look at annual patterns. If you sell seasonal products, you might notice a surge in sales immediately when the season is over. This happens because most buyers wait for end of season deals and offers. Using that information, you can prepare adequately for the next period and try to increase your sales.

How to Improve Search Rankings on YouTube

Using the metrics from YouTube analytics, you can do so much to improve your channel performance. Before you think of performance improvement, you must ensure your content and strategy are still in line with your goals and the audience's interests. Using this information, the next step is to learn about YouTube SEO. Any attempts at search engine optimization must always focus on delivering quality to the viewers. These are the people who engage with your content all the time, and if pleased, will share it within their network.

While the bottom line in optimization is to improve your performance and boost the financial angle of your work, boosting your channel or video performance will be fruitless if the content lacks value. Going through the YouTube analytics metrics, you should take a closer look at the trends and patterns you identify based on content value. If your content is on point, use the tips below to boost your search performance:

1. Abide by the rules

The first step to success online is to follow the rules. There are rules, regulations, and terms and conditions that govern how processes are run and promote fair practices. Remember that as much as YouTube allows you to post content and optimize as you wish, their core objective is to deliver the best experience to viewers and other stakeholders in the game. Their needs will always come first, and to ensure this happens, you must abide by the rules or risk your account being terminated.

YouTube has specific guidelines on how to use metadata. Read and keep them in mind when writing descriptions for your videos. There are lots of other content policies you must follow before uploading content to the platform. Most of the rules are common sense, so you should not have a difficult time.

2. Keyword use

Use Google Keyword Planner to find appropriate keywords for your videos. While going through the keywords, you should also perform a competitive analysis to determine the best keywords after seeing what other content creators use on similar content in your niche. Look at their video descriptions to see how the top-performing videos optimize their content, and do the same for your description.

Since YouTube allows you to use tags, you can also learn how to implement these for your videos. Tags are metadata fragments that determine how your videos show up in organic search. YouTube allows you to include up to 500 words of tags. For the best performance, use tags aligned to the topic of your video and your niche.

3. Upload frequently

It is no secret that YouTube currently trumps traditional TV, especially among the younger generation. That being said, like traditional TV, uploading content on a predictable schedule keeps audiences happy. Maintain your content schedule and upload videos frequently. The idea is to have an audience counting down the time until the next release on your channel. It is at this point that you know you are making progress on YouTube.

Apart from YouTube analytics, you can also use Google Analytics to learn how people engage with your channel, and more importantly, find out which videos drive the most traffic to your website. Google Analytics helps you track performance in two ways:

1. Track how YouTube visitors interact with your channel
2. Track the number of visitors who check your website from your YouTube channel

By tracking YouTube traffic, you will learn about your visitors, their location, and how they access your content on YouTube. You will also learn whether they have your videos on a playlist, or if they simply access your content from the way they sort videos. With lots of subscribers, this view provides insight into user engagement and can help you grow your channel.

First, you probably want to know how to track outbound traffic from YouTube to your website. For this, you must learn how people are finding your YouTube channel. To do this, you first isolate the traffic observed in Google Analytics. Set up filters so that your views can only show YouTube traffic. From this filter, you will see how audiences find your content, and their interaction once they land on your channel.

The information you gain from different analytics tools will help you learn how users find your channel, the best performing videos, and how you can meet your overall marketing goals and objectives.

Chapter 7:

Earning From Your

Content

One of the most difficult conversations to have with parents, baby boomers, and some Generation X folks is how you make money online. It is an unfathomable concept, yet millennials seem to be doing it so well. This concept is not just limited to the older folks, but anyone who thinks of investing in content creation will ask that question from time to time. People see you sitting in front of your camera and laptop for hours on end, and wonder how you get paid.

Let's put this into perspective. You are hooked on your favorite gaming channel learning tricks and tips on how to get past that difficult level you have been stuck on for weeks. You like the tips and think the uploader must be a genius. Well, they might be geniuses. They upload their content for free, right? So, how do they make money off it? Everyone starts by uploading their content online for free, rack up the numbers, and with time, they start earning. In this segment, we will focus on YouTube.

Content creators on YouTube earn somewhere between $0.01 and $0.03 for each view. This means that for every 1,000 views on your channel, you could earn up to $5. Your mind is probably doing the math on all the videos you watch that have millions of views, and deservedly so. There's so much money online and you are in the right place to learn how to earn it.

Curiously, while some content creators earn millions on YouTube, many others record insignificant earnings. What's the reason behind these differences? Primarily, ad blockers, ad quality, number of ad clicks, video length, and views are some of the key factors that determine how much you earn.

Do not be fooled by the number of subscribers on your channel, YouTube does not pay for that. However, growing your subscribers is important because your content shows up on their timelines frequently, increasing the chances that they will watch your videos. Subscribers are valuable because they will share your content, which will earn you more views and increase your chances of earning more.

YouTube will only pay you when you earn at least $100 from views. If you earn $5 for every 1,000 views, your content must earn at least 20,000 views to get paid. This is where the YouTube Partner Program comes in. Through this program, you can earn from ads placed on your page. We will discuss this program in the next section.

Your current YouTube status notwithstanding, there are three things you must figure out to help you get paid on YouTube. These are as follows:

1. Get the right equipment

Having covered this in-depth earlier, we will simply highlight that you must find proper lighting equipment, camera, and microphone to start your YouTube career on the right path.

2. Understand your niche

Niche marketing is about carving out a specialty from the mass market. Once you identify your niche, strike a rapport with your audience and use that to build a strong following. Some of the top niches include Instructables, life hacks, cooking, product reviews, gaming, celebrity gossip, and breaking news. You can also review some of the top YouTube earners each year to give you some inspiration on where to begin.

3. Post content frequently

All the top earners on YouTube post content regularly. The last thing you want is to create a sense of urgency and hunger for content in your audience and then fail to live up to the expectations. Since you cannot always upload at the same time all the time, you can create an upload schedule and inform your audience. Great video editing skills are a bonus. In case you are not so good at video editing, you can always outsource that part of your work to freelance video editors, or borrow a leaf from your book and learn from YouTube tutorials.

Starting out, you might not make as much to earn the millions that the top YouTubers earn, but by laying the right foundation, you will be on the right path.

YouTube Partner Program

The YouTube Partner Program (YPP) is a platform that gives you access to lots of features and resources to help you earn from YouTube. When you join the YPP, you have access to different monetization features, support teams for content creators, and a copyright match tool that helps you protect the integrity of your work. The eligibility criteria for joining the YPP is as follows:

1. You must adhere to all the monetization policies on YouTube
2. Reside in a country where the YPP is available
3. Link an AdSense account to your YouTube
4. Gain at least 4,000 public viewing hours over 12 months
5. Have at least 1,000 subscribers on your YouTube channel
6. You must enable 2-step verification on your Google account

Regarding viewing hours and subscribers, YouTube has to verify your content to determine whether it is suitable for audience consumption. This is also to verify whether your content meets the guidelines and policies outlined in the partnership agreement. Having signed the YPP terms, you will be notified when your account is eligible for monetization.

The process is straightforward, but not everyone who applies makes it to the YPP. Once your account is connected to an AdSense account, your application goes into a review queue. During this process, YouTube has human reviewers and automated systems that work together to determine whether you meet the requirements. If you meet the requirements and are accepted into the YPP, you can set up your preferences and customize your account for monetization. On the other hand, if you fail, this usually means most of your content failed the policies and guidelines test. You can, however, reapply after 30 days.

Once you join the YPP, you must keep uploading content regularly. This is important as YouTube seeks to create a sustainable and healthy ecosystem for users all over the world. If you do not upload a video or post to the Community tab for at least six months, YouTube can disable monetization for your account. This is not out of malice, but a way of ensuring that only the content creators who are actively engaged in, and bettering the YouTube community can enjoy the benefits.

As a responsible citizen, you have to find out the tax obligations in your country. YouTube will not be liable for any omissions or errors on your part in terms of filing tax returns or any other requirements in your country. Since earning online through platforms like YouTube is a new concept in many countries, you should follow up with your tax authorities for detailed guidance on compliance.

Product Merchandising

The misconception many people have about YouTube is that all the millions of dollars that top content creators earn come from ads. Relying on ad revenue alone might not get you that much money. Ads are just one of the revenue streams through which you can earn from your content. You can supplement the ad revenue by selling products.

Even though YouTube is a behemoth in the digital content market and the wide reach, most content creators agree that it should not be your ultimate option for monetization. Take the requirements for joining the YPP, for example. Gaining a thousand subscribers and up to 4,000 hours of content watched over a 12-month period translates to getting around 11 hours of your content watched daily. This is such a tall order.

Secondly, think of all the content creators joining the platform hoping to get paid, and the fact that YouTube keeps a huge chunk of your earnings. This clips your growth potential if you rely on YouTube for everything. Unless you are a celebrity or an influencer, earning solely from YouTube will stunt your growth.

The facts above should not discourage you from making the most of YouTube though. You can merchandise anything and promote it on YouTube. The concept here is to gain traction for your products, create conversations, and drive traffic to your website. Create quality content that adds value to your audience, get their attention then send them to your website. You can do this in the following ways:

1. Product reviews

Find some products relevant to your niche, use and review them. By evaluating such products, you give the audience a hands-on experience of what it means to use a certain product or subscribe to some service. The longer you do this, the more followers you will gain who are seeking similar experiences. As your community grows, you become an authoritative voice in that subject. Product reviews offer lots of opportunities for growth because more people will look for a review product if they have never heard of it yet, but wish to get the same experience you did.

2. Previews and teasers

Teasers are a good marketing tool because they give the audience an idea of what's coming. The best example of these are movie trailers. They create and build the hype around a product, creating anticipation around the release dates. The teaser content should show off some exciting aspects of the product.

Teasers and previews serve the same purpose but do not mean the same thing. Teasers are a collection of scenes in whichever order you please, complete with some dialog from the original content. Previews, on the other hand, show a scene from your content as it is. You can use either of these to create a discussion around your product.

3. Specialist reviews

This is similar to product reviews, with the only difference being that you bring experts to review products and services on your channel. Alongside the reviews, the audience will also benefit from expert tips and from time to time, insider information on hacks around the products reviewed.

Let's say you have a fitness channel on YouTube. You can invite some of the top fitness instructors you know to talk about fitness, nutrition, and anything else along that line that might help your audience learn something new from an expert. Through expert reviews, you will get more credibility to your name. If you are selling a product, you can also invite industry leaders to try and review your product on your channel.

4. Event marketing

Events create an interesting avenue to market your brand. Seek and attend events relevant to your product or service offering. You can sign up for any event from discussion boards to workshops and webinars. Record your engagement at these events and upload the content online. Events bost engagement by showing people interacting with your product and your brand. This hands-on experience will encourage more people to find out more about the products you sell.

5. Freemium content

Offering free content on YouTube and other video sharing platforms is a divisive approach. Some content creators swear by it, others feel it's a waste of time and resources. Of course, no one wants to give away their hard work for free. However, you don't have to offer everything for free. The idea here is to create two sets of videos, free and paid content. Share the free content widely to show audiences how amazing your work is.

Put as much effort into the free videos as the paid ones. Your audience will appreciate the consistency. Through the free videos, they get a glimpse of what it means to work with your brand, and if they love it, they would gladly pay for the premium content. Ensure your free videos offer or add value to your audience, and at the same time use the paid content to add more value.

Once you set up your content along these lines, you can start earning from your sales away from YouTube. By using YouTube as a platform to promote your content, you don't have to wait for 12 months or gain thousands of users to earn from your work. People who love your content will follow the links to your website and purchase your products or subscribe to your services.

To drive traffic back to your website, for example, your videos must include a call to action, encouraging the audience to check your website for more information, or direct them towards making a purchase. The videos should also make your brand visible vocally and visually with a compelling and clear message about the benefits they will receive from your content.

Affiliate Marketing on YouTube

Affiliate marketing is another way of making money off your YouTube channel. Through this mode, you include links in your videos and content that track purchases. Affiliate companies give you a personal link that they track for each purchase made from your channel. You earn commissions each time someone purchases an item through a link on your channel. Almost all the leading e-commerce stores and websites offer affiliate services, with Amazon being one of the most popular.

When setting up your platform, you can start with Amazon because of their sales volume, and the fact that it is one of the top options many people use. There are other affiliate networks like ImpactRadius.com and LinkShare.com where you can sign up and seek approval before you can apply for affiliate services.

Once you have the affiliate links, the next step is learning how to integrate them into your video. You can do this through product reviews. After discussing the product, share a link that customers can follow to buy the product. Apart from promoting content in this way, it is also one easy way to promote and monetize videos that are not sponsored. This type of marketing works best with content that you love, because customers will follow through and buy the products when they see your enthusiasm while reviewing the product.

Affiliate links are only effective if you use them well. Insert them right under the description. However, you also have to be careful not to insert too many links or your channel might look spammy. Besides, YouTube algorithms are written in such a way that they keep engagements in-house. The search engine optimization algorithms are written to encourage viewers to consume more content, watch as many videos and ads as possible without leaving YouTube.

The challenge is striking a balance between your affiliate needs and organic content growth on YouTube. If more people follow the links in your video, you will earn more from the affiliates, but your videos might not perform well on YouTube. You need to win on both fronts, so from time to time, you will have to choose which videos to upload for engagement and which ones to use for affiliate marketing.

With all the spam links and content available online, it is wise to inform the audience that you use affiliate links. This disclosure lets them know why they are important to your channel and builds trust because the viewers know what is required of them. When they watch your videos and enjoy the content, they would not mind supporting your affiliate program.

When signing up with affiliate networks, you also need to consider the commission rates. Each network has a different rate depending on the sales volume generated from your platform every month. Rates can start as low as 5% of sales depending on the advertiser. Make sure you read between the fine lines to understand the terms and conditions of their commissions to know whether you can comfortably work with them or not.

The bottom line about affiliate marketing is that you are getting paid for something that you would normally do for free. If you review products on your channel for free, why not start getting paid for it? While on the subject, remember that not all videos can be or should be sponsored. At times you just need to engage the audience and teach them a thing or two about a product.

Sponsored Posts

Have a look at these common phrases you see online from time to time:

1. Paid partnership with
2. Paid post
3. Affiliated with
4. Powered by
5. Sponsored by

These phrases indicate a given brand paid some money to bring the content to you. People generally remember and relate to branded content longer than normal advertisements. If you have a brand, promoting it on your podcasts, blogs, and videos will give you an advantage over other content creators.

If you are just starting out and do not have the resources to create your own campaigns, you can work with established companies and influencers by sponsoring their content on your videos. What is it about sponsored content that makes it stand out compared to traditional ads? To answer this, let's understand the concept of sponsored content. This is an approach where an advertiser pays for promotional content that is created and shared by an influencer, content creator, publisher, or another brand.

Engagement on sponsored content works best when you work with influencers or companies whose target aligns with your main audience, or one whose topics, products, or services are similar to your brand. Working along this line makes the concept more natural and feel less like an advertisement forced upon the audience.

If done correctly, sponsored content should leave your audience feeling like they learned something great, something that adds value to their lives. The benefit on your part is that it adds credibility and trustworthiness to your brand. Trust is a major factor that keeps audiences engaged through sponsored content.

Brands are always looking for content creators who can engage a large audience, and whose work is relevant to their target market. This is where your creativity will take you places. Here are some reasons why you should consider sponsored content:

1. Unlike traditional ads, sponsored content does not feel imposed. Instead of disrupting the user experience, sponsored content enhances it.
2. With sponsored content, you are not limited to one type of media or format.
3. It is a mutually beneficial form of marketing in that you receive funding from a brand, while the brand benefits from your audience that they can turn into customers.

Another reason why you can earn more using sponsored video content is that you spend more to create them, compared to Facebook posts and

Instagram stories, for example. The secret is to find an influencer marketing platform that aligns with your goals, like Klear or FameBit. Whichever way you go about it, you should always be transparent about your approach to your audience. The disclosure feature on YouTube, for example, informs your audience that you are advertising to them.

The concept of familiarity makes sponsored content work well for your audience. We develop preferences for brands the longer we are exposed to them. Think about this like the social media accounts you follow, shows you love to watch, or hobbies you enjoy.

Conclusion

Video marketing is everywhere. It has taken over social media and with billions of videos watched online daily, this is where you should be. Not so long ago video marketing was but a blip in content marketing, yet today every marketer worth their salt is focusing on video content. From leading brands to influencers, video is the in thing. The most important question is, are you doing it right?

Having gone through the chapters, you understand the value and role that audiences play in your video creation journey. The content channel might be yours, but all the crucial decisions depend on what works for your audience. You produce content for their consumption, and it is through their engagements that you will eventually monetize your content and make a steady income stream out of it.

Beyond the audience, other factors whose influence you cannot ignore are recording equipment, editing techniques, and resources. Looking at the cut-throat competition in content marketing, you have to start on the right note from the beginning. There is little room for error, so you cannot take chances. Besides, online audiences have had access to some of the best content over the years, so you can rest assured they will be less forgiving, and demand quality content regardless of whether you are a beginner or expert content creator.

Get the right equipment for the job. We outlined all the necessary tools and equipment you need to get started, including programs and apps. If your budget is strained, you can always start with the freemium offers and upgrade to the paid options as you scale up your project. Treat content creation with the same seriousness you would treat your regular job and you will have a better shot at success. Devote your time to it and commit the necessary resources. Don't just take it as a hobby project, your content creation gig is an investment into your future.

With all the tools, equipment, and resources necessary, everything comes full circle with personal skills. Everything else serves to prop your abilities. Are you a good storyteller? Can you write an engaging script? You should be able to impress, convince, and persuade audiences to see things from your perspective. Your narrative should be such that you put yourself in the audience's shoes. Where applicable, empathize and appeal to their innate needs. Establishing that personal connection with the audience gives your content a stronger appeal.

Creating engaging content might be a toil, but your work does not end when you hit the upload button. You must also go the extra mile and promote your content on social media. Learning some social media marketing skills will be of great help. Learn about search engine optimization, and how to promote videos on Facebook, Instagram, and any other platform where you can drive engagement with your audience.

Social media marketing will play a huge role in the success of your content. Since each social network has unique demographics, you should also understand their overall concept before pushing your content through them. You can promote your videos on all the social networks available, but the investment and resources you commit to each social network should be informed by how much value you can get from the network. By understanding the demographics of each of the social media outlets, you can leverage and position your content accordingly.

We mentioned how important it is to understand the dynamics of each video hosting platform before you upload your content on it. Once again, you have to follow the audience. A platform might be appealing to you, but not so much for your target audience. As we conclude this book, this is another factor that we cannot stress enough. For your content to succeed online and drive the engagement metrics you desire, ensure your plans align with audience needs, tastes, and preferences.

With all the tools at your disposal, you have what it takes to establish yourself as one of the best content creators in your niche. Videos are an amazing way to create interesting and engaging content that drives conversations online. This is the best time for you to research and find out what works for your audience. Ultimately, both yours and their goals must align.

Here's wishing you all the best in your content creation journey!

References

Ciampa, R., Go, T., Ciampa, M., & Murphy, R. (2020). *YouTube Channels*. John Wiley & Sons, Inc.

Cooper, P. (2020, February 20). *130+ Social Media Statistics that Matter to Marketers in 2019* (Hootsuite, Ed.). Hootsuite Social Media Management. https://blog.hootsuite.com/social-media-statistics-for-social-media-managers/

Drotner, K., & Christian Schrøder, K. (2010). *Digital content creation: perceptions, practices & perspectives*. Peter Lang.

Perkins, G. (2018). How to Start a Youtube Channel: Step-by-Step for Beginners. In *YouTube*. https://www.youtube.com/watch?v=AE6M3h chHnyw

Video Influencers. (2016). What Makes Good Content? 4 Tips for Making Great YouTube Content. In *YouTube*. https://www.youtube.com/watch?v=BQmDS OXYAIU